THE BLACK CHURCH IN THE U.S.

Its Origin, Growth, Contributions, and Outlook

by

William L. Banks

MOODY PRESS • CHICAGO

Library of Congress Catalog Card Number: 76-175492

ISBN: 0-8024-0870-2

Printed in the United States of America

Contents

Foreword

In this crisis hour in church history, *The Black Church in the U.S.* comes as a much needed work. This is a valuable book which commends itself to Christians on both sides of the color line.

The Reverend William L. Banks recounts the history of the black man and the black church in the U.S. with accuracy and honesty. It is evident that this work is a by-product of years of research. In times past, it was my privilege to hear the author speak on some of the subjects discussed in this book. I was elated as I read the manuscript. It does me good to see this work now available to everyone.

The writer's analysis of contributions and the growth of the black church in the U.S. is valid. Black Christians will learn much from this book, and at times be surprised to learn that all black preachers do not think alike! Moreover, white Christians and especially evangelicals, who have been *un*informed or *mis*informed on this subject, will have their eyes opened in the matter of race and Christian relations.

Mr. Banks, a Bible teacher, presents in a simple manner, clear-cut scriptural statements on many subjects that are being debated today by the black church. If the writer does a sequel to this work, I would like to see emphasis placed upon more recent contributions by black evangelicals.

It has been a privilege to read the manuscript of my former pastor. I commend the book to the reader, with the prayer that the Lord will give you a ready heart to understand the opened and burdened heart of the author.

KING A. BUTLER

Introduction

In recent days the number of "black studies" courses and books has proliferated. For the most part, books written on black religion have come from the pens of theological liberals, men outside the evangelical or conservative camp. However, doors also have opened to black Evangelicals; through their work more people are aware of the work of Christ in the hearts of Negro Americans. Out of the wilderness of materialism, antisupernaturalism, and the despising of Christianity as "the white man's religion," cry the voices of black men who are true to the faith "once delivered to the saints," and through their efforts others are made aware of the Negro's spiritual gifts, past and present contributions to the church, and his potential.

Black religion is relevant. In fact, such is the racial situation in America today that anything about the black man is relevant. W.E.B. DuBois said in 1903 that the problem of the twentieth century is the problem of the color line. Fifty years later, in 1953, he wrote:

> I still think today as yesterday that the color line is a great problem of this century. But today I see more clearly than yesterday that back of the problem of race and color, lies a greater problem which both obscures and implements it: and that is the fact that so many civilized persons are willing to live in comfort even if the price of this is poverty, ignorance and disease of the majority of their fellowmen; that to maintain this privilege men have waged war until today war tends to become universal and continuous, and the excuse for this war continues to be color and race.[1]

That the race issue looms large in the American mind today is impossible to successfully deny. Marks of identification such as natural or freedom haircuts, African- or quasi-

5

African-styled clothing, "Black and Proud" buttons and auto-mobile stickers are symbols of race identity as well as signs of race awareness. In the meantime, while blacks grow in self-knowledge, and while national magazines devote issues to *the* problem, racial "polarization" continues. The Sunday morning worship hour remains to a marked degree an hour of segregation. Slogans like "Black Is Beautiful," "White Is Right," "Black Power" and "White Backlash" stir up the emotions. Debates over open housing, contractual home sales, and school busing go on and on. Racial strife among our troops in both Germany and Vietnam troubles us. Boycotts, rioting, bombings, and assassinations continue, bearing evidence to the hatred existing between the races.

Contemporaneousness, however, is but one motivation for this study. There is also an appalling ignorance on the part of both blacks and whites concerning the religion of the American Negro, or concerning the American Negro, period. For too long history textbooks on practically every academic level have ignored, neglected or misrepresented the role of the black man in the United States. Many members of the majority feel they have no need to study the minority, and this unwillingness to learn about black men is in itself symptomatic. It is, in part, the by-product of arrogance and the feeling of superiority.[2] Thus, much of the criticism directed toward the American Negro, however valid and legitimate, is without sympathetic understanding. It is interesting that in a Harris Survey made in 1966, some 61 percent of white Americans felt that in general blacks were discriminated against; 28 percent felt blacks in general were *not* discriminated against. By 1969 some 46 percent believed Negroes were mistreated, but 43 percent felt they were not. This shows that the whites believe progress has been made. When specific areas were mentioned, such as decent housing, skilled-labor jobs, police treatment, and hotel and motel accommodations, the whites showed even less willingness to admit that discrimination exists. On the other hand, about 84 percent of the blacks believe they still face discrimination, showing that a very sizable gap exists between white and black thinking.

Increased knowledge of black history helps strengthen the Negro's concept of himself. Too many, for far too long, have been intimidated by the white world, kept in ignorance, and brainwashed into believing they were inferior. There is, then, therapeutic value in the black man's study of himself. One danger, of course, is pride. It does not take much for the Adamic nature in man to swing from a feeling of inferiority to an attitude of superiority.

Many Christians have allowed tradition and social customs rather than the Holy Spirit to influence them in the matter of race relations and attitudes. Quite possibly this study of black religion will help some white Christians to become more sympathetic and loving in their dealings with blacks, especially with Christian blacks. It is inconceivable that white Evangelicals will improve their image in the sight of the unregenerate black man if they refuse to have fellowship with Christian blacks. I have never cared much for the saying "Charity begins at home," mainly because too often I've heard it used by church members who refused to support foreign missions. But if it means Christians must learn to love other Christians before they can effectively demonstrate love to non-Christians, then I can better accept it.

These, then, are some of the reasons for this particular study: (1) more needs to be said from the black Evangelical's viewpoint; (2) it is relevant and contemporary; (3) there is a need to dispel ignorance; (4) it may help change some attitudes and concepts about blacks; and (5) above the readily accessible opinions and easily turned-on voices of the militants, black nationalists, radicals, and destructionists, we need to hear the voice of the God of all history, the Lord Jesus Christ, and see His hand moving, without respect of face or race, in the midst of the children of disobedience.

1

ROOTS: 1619-1776

The Portuguese and Spanish were the first Europeans to deal in the black slave trade. Rationalizing that it was God's will to bring black heathen into contact with Christianity, even if it meant a lifetime of enforced servitude, their ships carried slaves to labor in the Caribbean colonies as early as 1517. With the approval of their governments and the Roman Catholic church, the sellers of flesh maintained that "christianized" slaves were better off than free heathen.

Not all blacks who reached the shores of North America were slaves. Thirty blacks were with Balboa when he discovered the Pacific Ocean in 1513. Estevanico accompanied Cabeza de Vaca from Florida into Mexico during the years 1528-34. Other blacks were in this country prior to the institution of slavery.

Later the English, Dutch, and French entered the slave-trading picture by opening trading stations all along the heavily populated West African coasts. Still later the Americans entered, and by 1786 American and English ships carried the bulk of the trade. In the seventeenth century, slaves who were bought for almost $25 apiece in Africa were sold in the Americas for nearly $150. A ban on the slave trade later raised the prices and at an auction in Charleston, South Carolina, in the 1780s, a young girl sold for $1,000, with prices going up to $2,500 for a "trained" American-born craftsman, such as a carpenter, blacksmith, or mason.

Undoubtedly blacks were captured by whites. But it is also true that blacks sold blacks into slavery. When the Europeans first explored the African West Coast in the fifteenth and sixteenth centuries, they discovered slavery there a normal

9

practice among the natives. African kings had no scruples about selling black men into slavery. It was one way to deal with political rivals. Prisoners of war, criminals, debtors, and the kidnapped were the victims sold. As one rich king of Dahomey is reported to have remarked, "It is the custom of my ancestors; and if the white men come to buy, why should I not sell?"

AFRICAN RELIGION

Christianity was practically unknown below the Sahara in Africa prior to the sixteenth century when the Portuguese and Spanish began to establish missions on the West African coast. Black Evangelicals are not ashamed to admit the lost condition of the Africans sold into slavery; nor are we unmindful of the lost condition of the slave traders. But some blacks resentfully call Christianity the "white man's religion," boasting of the fact that the Africans had their own religion. Of course they had their own religion; but, like all others without Jesus Christ, they were hopelessly lost. There should be no reluctance in admitting the slaves' lost spiritual condition just because this factor is wrongly used to justify slavery.

African religions were polytheistic, and their highly developed priesthoods varied from tribe to tribe. They believed in nature gods, good and evil spirits, and in magic. Perhaps "ancestor worship" best describes the religion of these people. High mortality rates led naturally to time and thought concerning the estate of the deceased. This in turn led to ancestor worship.

It was believed that the spirits of their forefathers, deified upon death, lived on, taking an active interest in family affairs and maintaining unlimited powers over the living. These and other spirits dwelled in the family land, the mountains, rocks and trees in the community, and in the sky over it.

So the religion of the community was basically an attempt to placate these spirits, an attempt to stay on good terms with them. This way the worshiper would prosper. Anyone who could explain and answer questions about the unknown and make contact with these spirits obviously was an important part of this religion. And so there were sorcerers and witch doctors who practiced their magic, using powders, amulets, talismans, incantations, and sacrifice.

It is because the Animist has turned aside from the worship of the Life Giver that he finds himself a slave, in bondage to fear of evil spirits. This leads to the development of human mediums, who become possessed with a demon, and proceed to convey his message to those around. The witch doctor and sorcerer, the wizard and the magician are found among Animists everywhere.[1]

It is true that in parts of Africa the medicine men still practice their juju or voodoo. Like all other peoples, Africans have anxieties and need assurance and certainty in life. Whereas some sophisticated, godless Americans find relief in horoscopes and astrology, many Africans find relief in witchcraft. The role played by these practitioners of magic is not easily eliminated. Ignorance, superstition, fear, tradition, folklore, legend, and satanic influence combine to maintain the witch doctors' hold over the people. Despite laws passed by various African governments, black magic continues to weave its spell.

Slavery in the Caribbean and South America did not stop such practices. Perhaps this was because more Africans were shipped there than to the United States. But possibly the influence of the Roman Catholic church with its willingness to syncretize was partially responsible for continuing the witchcraft practice. The adaptation and mingling of heathen rites with what little the slaves learned about Christianity is best known as voodooism, and it still exists in Haiti, Jamaica, Brazil, and elsewhere in Latin America.

To what degree did the African religious practices prevail in this country? Slavery ended some of them, for African rituals were forbidden. Drums also were banned for fear they would be used to send messages and foment rebellion. Whatever spiritism there was, with its veneer of Christianity, later gave way to what might truthfully be called a Christian "Negro church."

THE MIDDLE PASSAGE

Nearly twenty million Negroes were made captive over the span of some 300 years (1517-1840). A more conservative estimate is 14.6 million. They were jammed and crammed into ships like sardines into a can and brought across the Atlantic, from the Gulf of Guinea to the New World, in a trip called the Middle Passage. It is estimated that perhaps 12 million landed in Latin America and about 2 million were brought to the United States. What happened to the other millions? Some died resisting capture; some died in captivity while being held in Africa waiting to be shipped out. Some committed suicide by eating quantities of clay. Others, beaten and too weak to continue the trek in the coffle (land convoy of slaves chained together), were abandoned to die. Most of the loss of life, however, came during the Middle Passage. Many that did reach the New World were not in the best of health. "Perhaps not more than half the slaves shipped from Africa ever became effective workers in the New World."[2]

Shackled in irons, they huddled beneath the decks for sixteen hours at a time in unbearable heat, filth, and stench, barely surviving on stale, spoiled food and stagnant water. During the several weeks it took to make the trip, the slaves were given only a few minutes a day on deck for fresh air and exercise. If the weather was bad they received neither fresh air nor exercise. Many died at sea from dysentery, smallpox, and other diseases. Some starved themselves to death, refusing to eat. To prevent this form of suicide, hot coals were applied to the lips to force the slaves to open their mouths to eat. Some committed suicide by jumping into the ocean. Others rebelled, especially those who were warriors taken in battle; often these were beaten or shot to death. And some died soon after reaching American soil.

The first black slaves to arrive in the United States were twenty who landed at Jamestown, Virginia, on August 20, 1619, from a Dutch frigate. Actually, these Africans were not slaves but indentured servants.[3] They were legally and temporarily bound Negro apprentices. Concerning these early black immigrants, A. H. Fauset said, "It is safe to assume that not one Negro in the original cargo of slaves . . . was a member of the Christian faith."[4] However, there is some evidence that they were baptized Christians who either were traded or pirated and transferred from a Spanish war vessel to a Dutch frigate. They could secure their freedom, and some did.

In 1787 there were nearly 700,000 Negro slaves here,

and about 59,000 free blacks. The proportion of Negroes to whites was at an all-time high of 19.3 percent in 1790. In the year 1808 there were about one million slaves and slightly more than 100,000 free. By 1830 there were slightly more than two million slaves, and 319,000 free. At the beginning of the Civil War there were almost four million slaves and some 488,000 free Negroes in America. Today, 1971, there are approximately 25 million black Americans.

COMPARISON WITH EUROPEAN IMMIGRANTS

Memories of Africa were erased. Family ties were destroyed. To safeguard against rebellion, members of the same tribe were separated, for without a common language there would be less chance of revolt. For economic reasons families were split up: a father sold to North Carolina, a mother and baby sent to Georgia, an older child delivered to a plantation owner in Virginia—never again to see one another.

Even though polygamy was practiced in Africa, every marriage was legal and a ceremony was performed. But here in America there was no legal marriage for the slave, with no ceremony; instead, there was, for the most part, promiscuity. The deleterious effect this had on Negro family life was tremendous and is still being felt today.

Slaves faced a different climate, a new environment, an unknown tongue. The uprooting, fear, and cruelty they experienced combined to make their life miserable. This is why it is difficult to keep silent when men boast of how their parents came to America, worked hard, and achieved success. If their parents succeeded, they conclude, the black man ought to be able to do likewise. With all due respect to the industry and perseverance of their white ancestors, and with due consideration of the hardships and discriminations many suffered, the fact remains: the black man in America was much more disadvantaged.

> Because of an inattention to history, the present day Negro is compared unfavorably with other racial and ethnic groups who have come to this country. Major differences in background are ignored. The black man was brought to this country forcibly and was completely cut off from his past. He was robbed of language and culture. He was forbidden to be an African and never allowed to be an American.[5]

Even the whites who were indentured or contract servants were able to change their condition of living. Owners of white slaves found them more difficult to handle and keep. Being white, these slaves could run away and mix with the majority population or settle down in new areas and escape detection. Blacks could not; they had no such control over their destinies. The Europeans who came to America, for the most part, brought with them an intact cultural background, skills, and education. If English was not their native tongue, at least they were able to communicate with someone who did speak their language.

These were not the only immediate advantages of the white immigrants. There was also no need for them to overcome the psychological stigma attached to slavery. There were, of course, white slaves, as mentioned above; some of these were former prostitutes, prisoners, and paupers who had been shipped to the United States and sold. However, one never hears boasting about such early American ancestry. There was no need to break out of an ironclad power structure built centuries earlier and calculated to keep them "in their place." And much credit should be given to the religious heritage they brought with them.

Not only did their white skin make their assimilation into the mainstream of American society easier; it also freed them from having to fight the evils born of so-called white supremacy and much of the lynching, disfranchisement, jim crow, and segregation based on race and skin color.

LITTLE PROGRESS MADE IN EVANGELIZATION

Obviously, in these early days of slavery, Christianity made little progress among the slaves. First, it was only natural that the new arrivals were slow to break away from African rituals which were a part of their way of life. Second, the slaves' general interest in religion was slight, and very little was done to encourage them to become Christians, even though "christianizing" these heathen was one of the earliest justifications given by Europeans for the slave trade. Failure to evangelize was in part traceable to the low spiritual state of the whites themselves. There simply were no strong evangelical churches in America at the time.

Third, there was the belief that conversion of the blacks

would make them unfit for slavery. Some felt that a slave was
no longer a slave when he became a Christian. Freedom, they
believed, was intrinsic to Christianity. The implied brotherhood and equality would pose a serious problem. Fourth,
the slaves' inability to read or understand English hindered
evangelism. Furthermore, if they learned to read, what would
stop them from reading books with ideas dangerous to the
status quo? Fifth, there were not enough missionaries to
cover the large but sparsely settled areas. Besides, travel was
difficult and whites who showed sympathy to blacks incurred
hostility from other whites. These and other factors combined
to make the total environment inconducive to the spreading
of the gospel.

> The history of the seventeenth century was that of relig-
> ious indifference to the Negro, with isolated exceptions. Lim-
> ited time, interest, money, personnel, and energy were spent
> in his behalf. . . . On the whole, religious leaders thought of
> the Negro as a little lower than a human being and consid-
> erably less than a member of the Church. As a rule, Negroes
> who were interested in religion had to be satisfied with the
> sacrament of baptism and whatever training was necessary
> to meet this requirement.[6]

2

REVIVAL: 1777-1819

THE PROTESTANT EPISCOPAL CHURCH

The eighteenth century brought a number of changes regarding evangelism among blacks. Fears that conversion meant freedom from servitude were allayed. Various legal rulings stated that Christianity was *not* a legal barrier to slavery. Feeling freer to evangelize, the denominations became busier.[1] The Anglican Society of the Propagation of the Gospel in Foreign Parts, founded in 1701 and intended to care for British emigrants, soldiers, officials, and merchants, soon turned its attention to American Negroes and Indians. Anglicans were the first Protestant missionaries to evangelize blacks. However, the necessity of knowing the Anglican creed, catechism, and ritual made it difficult to win over the black masses. Household slaves usually were more easily persuaded to accept this faith. But, with its rather high qualifications for the ministry, there was little chance of Negroes becoming active in the Anglican or Episcopal church. Anglicans were also the large slaveholders of the Atlantic Coast and were not as a church particularly evangelical or militantly missionary-minded. To this day there are no more than 80,000 Negro members in the Episcopal church.

Perhaps their attitude is best seen in the fact that the Anglicans were unwilling to allow their single black church, St. Thomas, to participate in their convention deliberations. St. Thomas was organized by Absalom Jones, who broke with Richard Allen because Jones did not believe the Methodist church welcomed Negroes. Dedicated in the year 1794 in Philadelphia, the church immediately applied for membership in the Episcopal Diocese of Pennsylvania. It was not accepted as a parish until 1865. The church still exists; in fact, of the twenty-eight Episcopal churches for Negroes, it remains the largest. In April, 1969, it held a six-month observance of its 175th anniversary. An interesting fact is that the original charter of St. Thomas limited the church's membership to black people. In 1965 the vestry decided to have the 1796 state charter changed, and by unanimous vote the parish opened its membership to all.

WORK OF THE VARIOUS DENOMINATIONS

During the latter half of the eighteenth century, about the time of the American Revolution, certain events occurred which helped to spread the Christian faith among the blacks. First, the inventions of the cotton gin, spinning and weaving machines, and the increased demand for cotton played a large part in the importation of more slaves. Southern soil was ideal for cotton, but more laborers were needed.

Second, and more important perhaps, the religious revival that took place from Maine to Georgia began to touch the lives of the blacks. Beginnings of this revival, called the Great Awakening, occurred in New Jersey in the 1720s with the preaching of a German named Frelinghuysen. Under the preaching of Jonathan Edwards, revival broke out in North-hampton, Massachusetts, in 1734-35. The Englishman George Whitefield was greatly used by God in his preaching missions to America. Mostly through Presbyterian and Con-gregationalist efforts, the Great Awakening spread throughout the colonies. However, after 1750 it was the Baptists who ex-perienced tremendous growth and influence among the com-mon people. As a result of the revival, the Methodists too, and to a lesser degree the Presbyterians, engaged in missionary work, and large numbers of Negroes were immediately at-tracted. The slaves were especially drawn to the Baptists and the Methodists.

While the Quakers had been in the forefront of the battle against slavery, very few blacks were attracted to them. Con-centrated in the North, they worked persistently with the free Negro, but the masses in the South remained untouched. Congregationalism, working later than some of the other de-nominations, confined its activity in large measure to the New England States, and so it also never came in contact with the masses of Negroes. Presbyterians were concentrated in areas where Negroes were scattered, so their influence was limited geographically.[2]

Slaves were drawn to the Methodists and Baptists because of the simplicity of service and the lack of ritual in these two groups. Their fiery message of personal salvation afforded a hope of escape from earthly sorrows. And because the Presbyterians, Episcopalians, and Congregationalists depended upon an educated ministry, their appeal to the Negro was limited. But the Methodist and Baptist preachers, for the most part, were not highly educated. Their preaching was ideally suited to the poor, the ignorant, the unlettered, the outcast—both black and white. The emotionalism and the feeling and fervor of their camp meetings and revivals gave the slaves a measure of social solidarity, providing the emotional outlet needed by an oppressed and enslaved people. Baptists were especially effective in winning the black man. Perhaps the fact that the church at first was confined to the plantation, thus restricting movement, played a large part in the establishment of the decentralized Baptists.

THE RISE OF THE NEGRO PREACHER

In time the black preacher played a significant role in the development of Negro life. The whites, of course, supplied the preachers most of the time in Negro churches during this era. And in white churches to which Negroes were allowed to come, white ministers preached. Occasionally Negro exhorters were allowed to speak from the floor (not from the pulpit). Some congregations had black preachers who became well known for their effectiveness. These were mostly free Negroes. In the North Lemuel Haynes was perhaps best known. Born in Connecticut in 1753, he grew to manhood in Massachusetts, served in the Revolutionary War, and later was licensed to preach in the Congregational Church. One of the first Negroes in America to pastor a white congregation, he served various churches in Vermont for more than twenty years. Samuel Ringgold Ward pastored a white congregation in Cortlandville, New York; Henry Highland Garnet served in Troy, New York. And there were others. Though without training and education, the natural ability and eloquence of these early Negro preachers opened doors. God's hand can be seen in this. Preaching was an outlet for leadership ability and it was an office of prestige. However, at this point the whites maintained control and kept close watch over the Negro preachers.

Three distinct types of churches coexisted during the slavery era: (1) white churches with blacks as members of the congregation, (2) separate black churches under white leadership and supervision, and (3) separate black churches with black leadership. Gradually the trend was toward the third group, separate and all black.

WHITE CHURCHES WITH BLACK MEMBERSHIP

Naturally, slaves attending the master's church was the first step. The first black converts attended the churches of those masters who permitted them to engage in any religious activity. Unfortunately, it was not so much a matter of expressing Christian brotherhood as it was an opportunity to keep an eye on the blacks. The slaves were not welcome, they were just tolerated, and that only if they were few in number. Whenever the number increased, certain provisions had to be made. For example, the back rows were for the slaves; they were not allowed to sit just anywhere. Sometimes the special section had a divider several feet high. In some churches the galleries were restricted for their use. Sometimes special services at different hours were held in the basement of a church. And it goes without saying that slaves often assembled in the churchyards and listened to the singing and preaching. So, in general, the first converts were allowed to attend white churches.

EARLY BLACK CHURCHES LED BY WHITES

Sentiment grew for separation from this system of inferiority, and more Negro churches were started. The increased number of blacks, the Negro's own desire for separation (although often only after it was made crystal clear he was not wanted)—these two factors helped to increase the number of Negro churches. Also keep in mind that many of the American churches were preoccupied with their own troubles; they were busy seeking separation from their European sponsors and the Negro's spiritual needs were shunted aside. However, in some cases whites helped establish churches for the blacks. The whites maintained supervision and also supplied the pulpit, but the lack of a sufficient number of white ministers to evangelize the many slaves was one of the chief difficulties of the black church with white leadership. Not that there were no Negro preachers at the time. There were some, but at this time they were rare, especially in the South.

In the years after the Revolutionary War, determined efforts were made for real independence—religious independence. The first distinctive Negro Baptist church in America was founded at Silver Bluff, South Carolina, between the years 1773 and 1775, by a white Baptist preacher, a Reverend Palmer. It is known that George Liele (or Lisle) preached there.[3] Liele was born a slave about 1750, probably in Virginia, and later taken to Georgia. Becoming a preacher, he was freed by his master in order to spend all of his time preaching.

One of Liele's slave converts was Andrew Bryan, who carried on the preaching ministry after Liele left America and settled in Jamaica. Bryan preached to both races. But at the end of the Revolutionary War the whites attempted to close the church; they whipped the members and, fearful of insurrection, imprisoned Bryan. As God would have it, Bryan's master supported him, and through the efforts of a white minister, Abraham Marshall, and a black minister, Jesse Peters, on January 20, 1788, the first organized Negro Baptist church in Georgia was established.[4] In 1792 a church was built in the suburbs of Savannah and called the First African Baptist Church. There is some confusion of dates, places, and names concerning these matters but the preceding account seems most accurate.

In 1776, Negro converts organized the Harrison Street Baptist Church in Petersburg, Virginia. Another church was founded in Richmond, Virginia, in 1780; one at Williamsburg, Virginia, in 1785; and the First African Baptist Church of Lexington, Kentucky, in 1790. In 1805, Joseph Willis, a free Negro, founded a Baptist church at Mound Bayou, Mississippi. A First African Baptist Church was established in 1809 by the Reverend Thomas Paul who later helped to organize the Abyssinian Baptist Church in New York City, of which former Congressman Adam Clayton Powell was the pastor. All of these came about through separation from white churches.

John Gloucester organized the First African Presbyterian Church in Philadelphia in 1807. The St. Thomas Protestant Episcopal Church, mentioned earlier, was organized by Absalom Jones in 1794. In 1818, Peter Williams became the first rector of the St. Philip's Episcopal Church in New York City. In 1829, in New Haven, Connecticut, the Dixwell Avenue Congregational Church was formed. And so the story goes. These separate churches played a tremendous role in developing Negro male leadership. Since the blacks could not participate in the politics of secular society, could not vote or hold office, possessed no social centers, and educational opportunities were limited, the church easily became the very center of Negro life.

NEGRO CHURCHES LED BY BLACKS

The third group, Negro churches with Negro leaders, also grew. At first the free blacks were mainly responsible for these independent assemblies; especially in the North was this true. Obviously the free Negroes in the North could do this, even though there were restrictions upon them:

> . . . there were all kinds of restrictive laws against free Negroes as regards voting, holding civic offices, testifying in court against white men, purchasing white servants, intermarrying with whites, and associating with slaves in the South. Free Negroes were required to pay taxes, however. In the North, political and economic conditions were somewhat better, but earning a living was more precarious than in the South.[5]

The 27,000 free blacks in the North in 1790 became nearly 250,000 in the year 1860. An almost equal number of free blacks were in the South, although in proportion to the total black population, more were in the North. Some had been born free; some bought their freedom; some ran away on their own; others were helped by the abolitionists and members of the Underground Railroad. Some were manumitted (given freedom by their masters). At any rate, in the North the Negro went further in setting up and establishing his own independent church.

Those Negro Baptists and Methodists in the North who were associated with white congregations began to increase in number, and the tension which resulted gave birth to independent black assemblies. Those in the South soon became quasi-independent. Whites, however, began to tire of playing religious nursemaid, and so more and more the black minister was allowed to lead. Many restrictions were no longer enforced so long as the slaves behaved themselves and did not plot to overthrow the social status quo. The taste of such freedom within the bounds of slavery was delicious; as restrictions were removed, the slaves relished the chance to enjoy their religion the way they wanted.

RICHARD ALLEN:
THE AFRICAN METHODIST EPISCOPAL CHURCH

The case of Richard Allen is an excellent example of the break with a white congregation. Born a slave in the city of Philadelphia, Allen was sold to a planter who took him to Delaware. He saved his money and bought his freedom in 1777, the same year that he was converted under Methodist preaching. Three years later Allen became a preacher and was greatly helped by a Bishop Asbury. When Allen proposed that a separate church be set up for the blacks, the idea was turned down by both races. However, when too many Negroes began to attend the St. George Methodist Episcopal Church in Philadelphia to hear Allen, who frequently preached there, the officials decided to segregate them. One day Allen, Absalom Jones, and William White occupied the "wrong" section of the gallery and while on their knees praying were pulled out of the church—a type of forerunner to the modern-day reaction to a "kneel-in." This prompted Allen and Absalom Jones to create the Free African Society, a benevolent organization, in April, 1787, and begin conducting their own religious services. In 1794, Allen founded the Bethel Church in Philadelphia which congregation became known as the Bethel African Methodist Episcopal Church; it is commonly called "Mother Bethel" by Negroes today.

The movement spread to Baltimore, Pittsburgh, and as far south as Charleston, South Carolina. In 1816 representatives met in Philadelphia to establish the African Methodist Episcopal church, and Allen became a bishop. In New York City a group of Negro Methodists left the John Street Methodist Church and in 1796 organized the African Methodist Episcopal *Zion* Church. This denomination was not a split from the AME church. From such beginnings both groups grew and increased their membership as independent Methodists. The Baptists established churches in Maryland, Virginia, Georgia, Kentucky, and in the northern cities of Boston, New York, Philadelphia, Cleveland, Cincinnati, Detroit and Chicago. Baptist influence at this time was not very strong because they were independent, decentralized churches which were not united in a denominational headquarters or national convention. That was to come later.

3

REACTION: 1820-1865

CAUSES BEHIND THE REACTION

In the critical era of 1820-65, slavery became an extremely important part of the South's economy. First, in the industrial revolution which took place, the invention of the cotton gin increased a slave's ability to clean cotton by fifty pounds a day. New machines like the wool-comber, spinning jenny, and steam engine played their part in increasing the slave's value. For those who stooped so low, slave-breeding became a lucrative practice. This had a great demoralizing effect upon the Negro, who had practically no family life as it was. New machines meant greater production; this required more slaves, who, in turn, became more valuable.

Second, there was a change in attitude toward slavery. Though Congress had passed a law in 1807 forbidding the African slave trade, smuggling continued, and laws against interstate kidnapping were violated. Groups which had formerly fought against slavery now began to approve of it and to change their message. However, other groups became even more militantly abolitionist. So the lines were drawn. Economics and racism won out. Thirty years before the Civil War, the Southern church became strongly pro-slavery. This radical switch held back the growth of the "Negro church."

Third, and perhaps most important, slave revolts struck fear in the hearts of many whites in the South. These rebellions, aided in some measure by the abolitionists, played a large part in turning the whites against the blacks. In 1822, Denmark Vesey, a free Negro carpenter working in Charleston, South Carolina, planned an extensive revolt but was betrayed by a house slave. Along with thirty-five or thirty-six others, he was hanged. The whites believed the black

24

Methodists were responsible for the plot and so Methodism came under fire, checking its growth in the Southern states. In 1831 Nat Turner led a bloody insurrection at Southhampton County, Virginia, killing some fifty-five whites before he and sixteen of his followers were captured and hanged. This revolt was attributed to Negro preachers brainwashed by white abolitionists.

RESTRICTIONS IMPOSED

The Southern states moved rapidly to enact stringent laws. In Mississippi in 1823 it became unlawful for six or more Negroes to meet for educational purposes. Meetings for religious purposes required the permission of the master. Even then a recognized white minister or two reputable whites had to be present. In Delaware in 1831, no more than twelve blacks were allowed to assemble later than 12 o'clock midnight unless there were three respectable whites present. The law stated also that no free Negro should attempt to call a meeting for religious worship unless authorized by a judge or justice of peace upon recommendation of five respectable white citizens. In many sections of the South, Negro preachers were silenced and not allowed to preach other than on their own plantations, and then only with their masters' consent. Paul Laurence Dunbar delightfully captures in his poem, "An Ante-Bellum Sermon," the guardedness, apprehension and alertness of the Negro preacher delivering a sermon under circumstances such as prevailed during this period.

AN ANTE-BELLUM SERMON

We is gathahed hyeah, my brothahs,
   In dis howlin' wildaness,
Fu' to speak some words of comfo't
   To each othah in distress.
An' we chooses fu' ouah subjic'
   Dis—we'll 'splain it by an' by;
"An' de Lawd said, 'Moses, Moses,'
   An' de man said, 'Hyeah am I.' "

Now ole Pher'oh, down in Egypt,
   Was de wuss man evah bo'n,
An' he had de Hebrew chillun
   Down dah wukin' in his co'n;

'Twell de Lawd got tiahed o' his foolin',
    An' sez he: "I'll let him know—
Look hyeah, Moses, go tell Pher'oh
    Fu' to let dem chillun go."

"An' ef he refuse to do it,
    I will make him rue de houah,
Fu' I'll empty down on Egypt
    All de vials of my powah."
Yes, he did—an' Pher'oh's ahmy
    Wasn't wuth a ha'f a dime;
Fu' de Lawd will he'p his chillun,
    You kin trust him evah time.

An' yo' enemies may 'sail you
    In de back an' in de front;
But de Lawd is all aroun' you,
    Fu' to ba' de battle's brunt.
Dey kin fo'ge yo' chains an' shackles
    F'om de mountains to de sea;
But de Lawd will sen' some Moses
    Fu' to set his chillun free.

An' de lan' shall hyeah his thundah,
    Lak a blas' f'om Gab'el's ho'n,
Fu' de Lawd of hosts is mighty
    When he girds his ahmor on.
But fu' feah some one mistakes me,
    I will pause right hyeah to say,
Dat I'm still a-preachin' ancient,
    I ain't talkin' 'bout to-day.

But I tell you, fellah christuns,
    Things'll happen mighty strange;
Now, de Lawd done dis fu' Isrul,
    An' his ways don't nevah change,
An' de love he showed to Isrul
    Wasn't all on Isrul spent;
Now don't run an' tell yo' mastahs
    Dat I's preachin' discontent.

'Cause I isn't; I'se a-judgin'
    Bible people by deir ac's;
I'se a-givin' you de Scriptuah,
    I'se a-handin' you de fac's.

Cose ole Pher'oh b'lieved in slav'ry,
   But de Lawd he let him see,
Dat de people he put bref in,—
   Evah mothah's son was free.

An' dah's othahs thinks lak Pher'oh,
   But dey calls de Scriptuah liar,
Fu' de Bible says "a servant
   Is a-worthy of his hire."
An' you cain't git roun' nor thoo dat,
   An' you cain't git ovah it,
Fu' whatevah place you git in,
   Dis hyeah Bible too'll fit.

So you see de Lawd's intention,
   Evah sence de worl' began,
Was dat His almighty freedom
   Should belong to evah man,
But I think it would be bettah,
   Ef I'd pause agin to say,
Dat I'm talkin' 'bout ouah freedom
   In a Bibleistic way.

But de Moses is a-comin',
   An' he's comin', suah and fas'
We kin hyeah his feet a-trompin,
   We kin hyeah his trumpit blas'.
But I want to wa'n you people,
   Don't you git too brigity;
An' don't you git to braggin'
   'Bout dese things, you wait an' see.

But when Moses wif his powah
   Comes an' sets us chillun free,
We will praise de gracious Mastah
   Dat has gin us liberty;
An' we'll shout ouah halleluyahs,
   On dat mighty reck'nin' day,
When we'se reco'nised ez citiz'—
   Huh uh! Chillun, let us pray![1]

    The Negro preachers were thus restricted by law on the basis of being incompetent, abusing their office, disturbing the peace, and influencing the breaking of the law and creating unrest.

Because the church was instrumental in the education of the slaves, these restrictions served to arrest educational advancement and to compound ignorance. By 1834 Sabbath schools restricted their training to oral instruction, and in 1840 it is reported that only fifteen Negro Sabbath schools existed in the South, with 1,459 pupils attending. The education of the Negro in the South was brought virtually to a standstill. It had not been much to begin with, but now it was prohibited by law or discouraged by white mobs. Although efforts were made to prevent white Northerners from coming in to teach the Negroes how to read and write, some risked their lives to do so anyway. Throughout American Negro history, no matter how brutal and evil the minority of whites, or how indifferent the majority, there were always those few brave souls who sought to alleviate the black man's misery and dispel his ignorance. If any black man thinks his race had it bad, let him rest assured it would have been much worse had it not been for some genuine, humanitarian, Christian whites.

In summary, the increased demand for cotton, the increased value of the slave, along with the fear of revolts, helped change the attitudes of many whites toward the black man and slavery. The early nineteenth century saw great restrictions placed upon black religion in the South. Between the years 1820 and 1865, Negro religious life in the South was proscribed by the outlawing of Negro preachers in many areas; blacks were made to attend their masters' churches, and it became a crime to teach blacks to read or write.

A TERRIBLE DEMORALIZING ERA

Without doubt slavery helped to produce shiftlessness, lack of reliability, and the attitude of give the least and get the most in the slaves.

> Under the lax moral life of the plantation, where marriage was a farce, laziness a virtue, and property a theft, a religion of resignation and submission degenerated easily, in less strenuous minds, into a philosophy of indulgence and crime. Many of the worst characteristics of the Negro masses of today had their seed in this period of the slave's ethical growth. Here it was that the Home was ruined under the very shadows of the church, white and black; here habits of

shiftlessness took root, and sullen hopelessness replaced hopeful strife.²

Cut off from the light of God's glorious gospel, the black man's old nature had a field day. Lying, cheating, stealing, brutality, sexual immorality—all increased. Loafing on the job, pretending to be sick in the field or on the auction block itself, destroying crops, killing animals, burning houses— these were but a few of the ways in which slaves showed their hatred for slavery. Undoubtedly Negroes learned to lie to white men while living in a perpetual state of insurrection suspicion. Fear helped many to develop the capacity to mask their true feelings.

Only here and there could one find a slave with an intelligent view of Christianity. It is estimated that of the 2, 245,144 slaves in America in the year 1835, only 245,000 had a saving knowledge of Jesus Christ.³ What else could be expected with so much against them? If the white slave masters were hypocrites, or even if they were sincere, what but a bad effect could their actions have on slaves who considered these masters Christians? It was during this period that many efforts were made to provide a scriptural basis for justifying slavery and segregation.⁴ Attempts to make the black man further inferior were nothing new, having begun years earlier in the colonies, but during these decades prior to the Civil War the supporters of slavery waxed eloquent.

THE HAMITIC CURSE

One belief held by many during this period was the "Hamitic curse," and Genesis 9:25 was a favorite text of many Southern preachers. A study of Genesis 9:20-27 reveals that it was Ham, the father of Canaan, who saw Noah's nakedness. However, the curse is upon Canaan, Noah's grandson. Because the Bible does not teach that curses fall indiscriminately upon the heads of the innocent, different solutions have been offered as to why Canaan and not Ham was cursed. Some have suggested that the words "his younger son" (v. 24), meaning "the little one," could refer to Canaan as well as to Ham, thus punishing Canaan for his own sin and not that of his father. One thing is clear: those who talk about the Hamitic curse must remember that Canaan, not Ham, was cursed. If Ham bore blame, we are unaware of his punishment. It is simply prophesied that the moral guilt of Ham would manifest itself in Canaan and his descendants. Thus, first of all, it was Canaan, not Ham, upon whom the curse fell.

Second, the other three sons of Ham—Cush, Mizraim and P(h)ut—were not cursed. A study of the migration of the descendants of Ham reveals they went not only to Egypt and Ethiopia, but to the land of Canaan or Palestine.[5] The Babylonians, through Nimrod, are descendants of Cush (Gen 10:8-10.) These people were *not* Negroes and, whatever their subjection or subjugation to Shem (9:26) and Japheth (9:27), it had nothing to do with skin color.

Third, in Joshua 3:10 is found the preface of the struggle against the Canaanites who were finally defeated in David's day. The curse should be dropped right there and not extended to all of Ham's descendants.

Segregationists today do not use the Bible to support their beliefs as much as was done by the segregationists of the period under study. Today they give social reasons, or talk about a culture gap, crime, IQ, and immorality. But during these pre-Civil War days, the Bible was woven into the very fabric of the system defending slavery. Buswell states concerning the so-called Hamitic curse: "It is stock teaching about the Negro from far more Northern pulpits than is sometimes realized."[6] To be sure, there are still those who believe the black man is doomed to be a hewer of wood and drawer of water (Jos 9:23).

NEW TESTAMENT SCRIPTURES AND SLAVERY

Not only were scriptures cited in an attempt to support the belief that Negroes were cursed, but they were used to support the very institution of slavery itself: See Ephesians 6:5-9; Colossians 3:22-25; 1 Timothy 6:1-2; Titus 2:9-10; 1 Peter 2:18-19; and Philemon. Concerning the Pauline passages, Howard Thurman tells of his grandmother who said,

> During the days of slavery the master's minister would occasionally hold services for the slaves. Old man McGhee was so mean that he would not let a Negro minister preach to his slaves. Always the white minister used as his text something from Paul. At least three or four times a year he used

as a text: "Slaves, be obedient to them that are your masters . . . as unto Christ." Then he would go on to show how it was God's will that we were slaves and how, if we were good and happy slaves, God would bless us. I promised my Maker that if I ever learned to read and if freedom ever came, I would not read that part of the Bible.[7]

There are still those today who claim these passages teach a maintaining of the status quo, and that they are the thoughts of an unenlightened age. Black Muslims say these scriptures were given to the Bible-idolizing slaves to help keep them docile and harmless. These critics fail to realize that this gospel—though it includes obedience to the powers that be—undermines slavery and all other wicked institutions.

Hotheads and black militants see the Bible way as too slow. Apparently they neither know nor care that had Christ or Paul struck out explicitly against slavery, the inevitable result would have been the end of their ministries. The social turmoil caused by such actions would have been inconsistent with their ultimate purposes—Christ's, to die on the cross of Calvary at the proper time on God's clock; and Paul's, to preach the unsearchable riches of the crucified, buried and risen Saviour in those areas of Asia Minor and Europe to which the Holy Spirit would lead. I firmly believe that if our slave grandparents had acted as some of today's black militants desire to act, they would have gone the way of the American Indian, and it is quite possible these black militants would not be here today. Obedience to the Bible on this issue has, in part, insured the black man's survival in America.

The Bible's comparative lack of interest in the social fact of slavery is not based on eschatological hope or otherworldliness alone. Rather, the New Testament emphasis is on the fact that all men, slave or free, need Christ, and that a Christian should live for Jesus Christ in whatever state he is found (1 Co 7:20 f.). Despicable as slavery is, a person's attitude toward God and his relationship to Him take precedence over slavery and all other relationships, be they racial, cultural, or social. External freedom is valuable indeed, but its value fades into nothingness when compared with freedom from self and the practice of sin. Yet, in view of all this, it remains true that the way in which slaves were integrated into the Christian community accords with the manner in which Jesus, and indeed the New Testament as a whole, thought and spoke of them. If slavery was not rejected from the Christian standpoint, every effort was made to bring it to an end. . . . The rule of love . . . is rooted in the fact that all members of the community stand in the same relationship to Christ and are thus united on the same level in Him. It is obvious that this must finally lead to abolition of slavery among Christians.[8]

EVENTS LEADING UP TO THE CIVIL WAR

By the 1850s, cotton had become king, accounting for nearly half of the total value of our exports. And the black man who worked the cotton had become a great divider of men. Things were heading toward a climax in the 1850s and, as time wore on, turbulence increased. Deciding which states would become free of slavery was a problem. Slave owners and abolitionists were at each others' throats. The novel *Uncle Tom's Cabin,* by H. B. Stowe appeared in 1852 and had a tremendous impact against slavery. The Dred Scott decision of the Supreme Court was handed down in 1857. Scott, taken to free territory by his master, filed a lawsuit for his freedom, but the court denied it, claiming he could not sue because he was not a citizen.

Near the end of the decade, in 1859, the fanatic John Brown led a rebellion, was captured, tried for treason, and hanged. Then in 1860, Lincoln was elected President. What a decade! North and South had been brought to an emotional pitch never before reached. Soon the sparks that smoldered for more than two hundred years would burst into flames and engulf the entire nation. We have seen the vital role played by the black man in this country's history. Surely the institution of slavery affected every aspect of American life. It is inconceivable that a course in American history can be taught with this matter of the black man's role ignored, overlooked, or played down. This is not to say that everybody owned slaves. The vast majority of the Southern whites did *not*. When the Civil War began, approximately 385,000 of the 7 million whites held slaves, and 88 percent of these slave owners had fewer than twenty slaves each. Yet, it must be understood that the institution of slavery profoundly influenced every phase of American life.

4

RECONSTRUCTION AND RETALIATION: 1866-1914

JIM CROW

If the material which has been covered thus far in this text could be entitled "Slavery to Freedom," the next section, embracing the Civil War to World War I, can be called "Freedom to Jim Crow." *Jim Crow* is a slang term for the post-Civil War practice of systematically segregating and suppressing the American black man. It was the successful attempt by whites to shackle the freed blacks and to establish a permanent caste system based on race. Jim Crow was a character in a play by Thomas D. Rice who died in 1860.[1] In the play, performed in a New Orleans theater, the Negro folk-nonsense ballad was sung by a Negro cripple who flopped about the stage imitating the motions of a crow. It was such a success that black-faced comedians of both races all across the country tried their hand at it. The term probably came to have its present meaning because it describes the Negro crippled by the many segregation laws established at this time.

THE RECONSTRUCTION PERIOD: 1866-1877

Freed by the Emancipation Proclamation, Negroes found themselves far from enjoying equality. True, in those restless days immediately following the Civil War, commonly called "Reconstruction," many blacks held positions of prominence and power. In fact, in the early 1870s, seven Negroes were in Congress at the same time. A total of twenty were elected to the House of Representatives during this era; two were preachers.

Nonetheless, such progress was short-lived. The feeling of inferiority had been stamped deep into the souls of black folk for more than two hundred years and impressed, according to some, with God's sanction and approval. Such feeling is not a thing overcome at the snap of a finger or the signing of a piece of paper. Nor could anything the President proclaimed change the hearts of evil white men. Unfortunately, many who fought for the rights of black men (abolitionists and others) soon forgot about the Negro's plight after the war.[2] Reconstruction ended with the shameful Compromise of 1877, when Republican politicians gave up all the moral purpose with which they had supposedly fought the Civil War in return for Southern Democratic support of Northern industrialists. Federal troops were withdrawn, leaving the freed blacks with virtually no protection from defeated, vindictive Southern whites. Bitterness gave birth to the abominable Ku Klux Klan. Violence and new laws combined to enforce racial segregation. Black politicians were weeded out and measures taken to see that none would be elected again. Indeed, none were for nearly one hundred years, until in 1963 a black man was elected to the legislature of the state of Georgia.

Black men were slowly disfranchised when qualifications for voting were set up which they could not meet: poll taxes, literacy tests, previous voting record, the "grandfather clause," knowledge of the Constitution, etc. Statistics for the state of Louisiana sum up what happened elsewhere: in 1896 there were 130,334 Negroes registered to vote; in 1904, only 1,342. In 1896 the Supreme Court came out with its famous "separate but equal" facilities decree and set the pattern for racial separation for more than fifty years.

TREMENDOUS CHURCH GROWTH

But what about the church? How did it fare? It grew by leaps and bounds and easily became the very center of Negro social life: a means for self-expression, recognition, and shelter from the cruel white world. Many mutual-aid societies and orders were founded which, along with the churches, offered help in time of sickness and death. The Negro preacher became a very important factor in the life of his people, more so than ever before. Two things happened. The "invisible" church of the Southern plantations during slavery time now became visible, adding for the most part to the size and number of independent Baptist and Methodist Negro churches. Second, free Negroes—those who had been free prior to the Emancipation Proclamation—in the North redoubled their efforts to break away from what they regarded as an inferior relationship with white churches. In short, these days immediately following the Civil War were marked by a notable trend toward establishing independent, all-black churches. Negro preachers were now no longer silenced, their churches no longer proscribed by laws of the South. So the Negro began to withdraw from the white churches. And the invisible merged with the visible.

THE METHODISTS

Black Methodism had been unable to expand in the South because the whites blamed the Denmark Vesey rebellion in South Carolina in 1822 upon the black Methodists and this hindered the denomination's expansion in the South. Then, too, the itinerant ministry with traveling officers was simply an impossibility for Negroes, whether bond or free. However, with Emancipation they were free to move about and evangelize. Consequently, after the Civil War, many Negro Methodist assemblies came into existence and all grew very rapidly.

The AMEZ (African Methodist Episcopal Zion), begun in 1796 in New York City, had great growth after the Civil War. Between the years 1860 and 1870 it grew from 26,746 members to about 200,000 members. By 1880, fifteen annual conferences had been organized in the South. As for the AME church, it had only 20,000 members in 1856, and 75,000 by 1866. By 1876 there were more than 200,000 members; and in 1880 the organization claimed a membership of some 400,000, most of whom were freed men in the rural South. The influence and material wealth of the AME church increased proportionately.

A third major Negro Methodist group was born during this period. At the end of the Civil War there were slightly more than a quarter million Negro members of the Methodist Episcopal Church, South. The word *South* is added because the white Methodists split in 1844 over the question of slavery. Southern Negroes continued to join and worship in the churches of their masters. In the North, as mentioned earlier in connection with Richard Allen, there were Negro assemblies still connected with the Methodist Episcopal church. After the Civil War, in 1866, Negro members of the ME Church, South, were permitted to organize a separate body. Dissatisfied with segregation and racial restrictions of the ME Church, South, they were set apart. In December, 1870, at Jackson, Tennessee, a special Negro conference was convened by the white bishops, under orders from the general conference.

Separation was recommended, and the Colored Methodist Episcopal Church was born. Some 70,000 black communicants were transferred from the old to the new organization, two Negro bishops invested, arrangement of property division made, and by the year 1886, only 527 Negroes remained on the rolls of the parent church.[3] In 1956, the word *Colored* was changed to Christian. Interestingly, the Southern ME Church still has fellowship with the CME Church and assists in organizing and operating its educational program.

THE BAPTISTS

Prior to the Civil War the Baptists were composed almost entirely of local congregations, but they had attracted more Negroes in the South than had other denominations. After the Civil War they enjoyed phenomenal growth and quickly became the most numerous. A total membership in 1850 of 150,000 became nearly 500,000 by 1870. Independent local churches sprang up overnight. Since there was no educational requirement, all who felt the "call" to preach let it be known. Said Booker T. Washington,

> In the earlier days of freedom almost every colored man who learned to read would receive "a call to preach" within a few days after he began reading. At my home in West Virginia the process of being called to the ministry was a very interesting one. Usually the "call" came when the individual was sitting in church. Without warning the one called would fall upon the floor as if struck by a bullet, and would lie there for hours, speechless and motionless. Then the news would spread all through the neighborhood that this individual had received a "call." If he were inclined to resist the summons, he would fall or be made to fall a second or third time. In the end he always yielded to the call. While I

wanted an education badly, I confess that in my youth I had a fear that when I had learned to read and write well I would receive one of these "calls"; but, for some reason, my call never came.[4]

Obviously, the ministers who established these local Baptist assemblies were for the most part unlettered. There was no hierarchy or centralized authority. Each church was its own sovereign body; there was not then and is not now any such thing as *the* "Baptist Church." This lack of centralization meant that the Baptists were initially not nearly as strong and influential as the better-organized AME Church. Nonetheless, with freedom came the organization of larger Baptist bodies or conventions. In 1866 the Negro Baptists established their first state convention in North Carolina. In 1867 Alabama and Virginia followed suit. By 1870 every Southern state had a Negro Baptist Convention. To the distress of Negro leaders, in many localities whites sought to control these Negro Baptist associations and conventions.

In 1867 the Consolidated American Baptist Convention was organized; it continued until 1880. Then, in Montgomery, Alabama, in 1880 a convocation representing various Southern Negro Baptist churches, associations, and state conventions established the Foreign Mission Baptist Convention of the USA. In Atlanta, Georgia, in 1895 this convention and the American National Baptist Convention of 1880, and the American National Educational Convention of 1893, combined and became the National Baptist Convention of the USA. It was incorporated in 1915 with 3 million members. Today it is the largest single denominational convention of Negro Christians in the world, claiming 6.4 million members.

FRUSTRATING SECULAR CONDITIONS
FORCE CHURCH STRUCTURING

The years 1865-1914 are often considered the worst period in the American Negro's history. One writer referred to this period as

the silent era, a time in which even those churches which had vociferously championed the abolition of slavery largely ignored the racial problems gathering during these years and turned their backs on the liberated slaves. (It is not coincidental that this was also the era of a vigorously expanded

Protestant foreign mission program—a possible compensa-
tion abroad for a glaring default at home). In this era the
North, preoccupied with its rapid industrial development,
not only neglected the Negro it had freed and left him to
flounder but also in a nationwide political maneuver returned
the Negro to the control of his former master and to a condition little better than his previous slavery.

The silent churches tacitly and passively complied with the
national mood. Many of the evils which haunt race relations
today arose not in slave days but in the early years of that
period in which the North betrayed the man it had freed,
"selling" the Negro once more to the South to discharge a
burden and to gain political leverage.[5]

Kenneth Clark described this period as the "nadir" of the
Negro in American life. It came, he said,

as a seemingly abrupt and certainly cruel repudiation of the
promises of Reconstruction for inclusion of the Negro into
the political and economic life of the nation. This was a
period when the white crusaders for racial justice and democracy became weary as the newly freed Negroes could no
longer be considered a purely Southern problem; when the
aspirations for and movement of the Negroes toward justice
and equality were curtailed and reversed by organized violence and barbarity perpetrated against them; when as a result of abandonment and powerlessness, the frustrations, bitterness, and despair of Negroes increased and displaced op-
timism and hope.

This period culminated in the institutionalization of rigid
forms of racism—the enactment and enforcement of laws re-
quiring or permitting racial discrimination and segregation
in all aspects of American life. This retrogression in racial
democracy in America was imposed by white segregationalists
with the apathy, indifference, or quiet acceptance of white
liberals and moderates who served as necessary accessories.[6]

It was during this period that the invisible merged with
the visible: the hidden plantation church integrated with the
church of the free Negro. Negro life was organized and
structured as never before. The influence of this period cannot be overestimated. Whatever organized social life there
had been for the slaves in Africa was destroyed by their
slavery in America. Their plantation living was such that a

structured family life was nigh impossible. Fear of insurrection was one reason that whites prohibited blacks from organizing their religious life. Thus, outside of their different roles or tasks on the plantation itself, there was no organized social life.

But when the blacks were freed, things changed, and the blending together of the invisible slave church with the free Negro church helped to provide some organization in Negro life. Writing in 1903, DuBois summarized:

> The Negro church of today is the social center of Negro life in the U.S., and the most characteristic expression of African character. Take a typical church in a small Virginia town: it is the "First Baptist"—a roomy brick edifice seating five hundred or more persons, tastefully finished in Georgia pine, with a carpet, small organ, and stained-glass windows. Underneath is a large assembly room with benches. This building is the central club-house of a community of a thousand or more Negroes.
>
> Various organizations meet there,—the church proper, the Sunday School, two or three insurance societies, secret societies, and mass meetings of various kinds. Entertainments, suppers, and lectures are held besides the five or six regular weekly religious services. Considerable sums of money are collected and expended here, employment is found for the idle, strangers are introduced, news is disseminated and charity distributed. At the same time this social, intellectual, and economic center is a religious center of great power.
>
> Depravity, Sin, Redemption, Heaven, Hell, and Damnation are preached twice a Sunday with much fervor; and revivals take place every year after the crops are laid by; and few indeed of the community have the hardihood to withstand conversion. Back of this more formal religion, the Church often stands as a real conserver of morals, a strengthener of family life, and the final authority on what is Good and Right. Thus one can see in the Negro church today, reproduced in microcosm, all that great world from which the Negro is cut off by color prejudice and social condition.[7]

FAMILY LIFE

As already mentioned, prior to enslavement the Negroes' African forebears practiced polygamy, but it was still a type of marriage—legal and useful in stabilizing society. But as slaves in America there was neither legal nor religious sanction of marriage. Promiscuity is perhaps the best word to describe the moral situation. Another development which took place in slavery was the creation of the matriarchy. Circumstances of the times helped to create a society which centered around the mother or some other woman on the plantation. As it was, male and female just mixed together and any children born of these unions usually remained with the mother.

The father was just a visitor; he was without legal or recognized status. In general, the white slave masters had little regard for mother-child relationships and practically no regard for father-child relationships. It meant nothing to snatch away a man and sell him elsewhere. Even where the father attempted to remain loyal to his mate and children, there was the threat that he would be separated and sold elsewhere. Here is the way one writer put it:

> The plague-spot in sexual relations is easy marriage and easy separation. This is no sudden development, nor the fruit of Emancipation. It is the plain heritage from slavery. In those days, Sam, with his master's consent, "took up" with Mary. No ceremony was necessary, and in the busy life of the great plantations of the Black Belt it was usually dispensed with.
>
> If now the master needed Sam's work in another plantation or in another part of the same plantation, or if he took a notion to sell the slave, Sam's married life with Mary was usually unceremoniously broken, and then it was clearly to the master's interest to have both of them take new mates. This wide-spread custom of two centuries has not been eradicated in thirty years.
>
> Today Sam's grandson "takes up" with a woman without license or ceremony; they live together decently and honestly, and are, to all intents and purposes, man and wife. Sometimes these unions are never broken until death; but in too many cases family quarrels, a roving spirit, a rival suitor, or perhaps more frequently the hopeless battle to support a family, lead to separation, and a broken household is the result. The Negro church has done much to stop this practice, and now most marriage ceremonies are performed by the pastors. Nevertheless, the evil is still deep seated, and only a general raising of the standard of living will finally cure it.[8]

The constant shifting around and general uncertainty accelerated sexual promiscuity. More than one hundred years after Emancipation, the effects of such moral looseness are still felt. Common-law living is still a problem some Negro ministers have to deal with in their congregations.

LACK OF A PROPER MALE IMAGE

The high degree of mobility in the slave trade accentuated the moral vacuum. This, combined with the lack of self-respect felt by men who had little or no opportunity to constructively express their manhood, further lessened the black man's role. Being head of the home should not create pride or feelings of superiority in the male. Rather, it is a matter of function. God made Adam first, not Eve. After the fall, Eve was told, "Thy desire shall be to thy husband, and he shall rule over thee" (Gen 3:16). Centuries later the apostle Paul said women were not to usurp authority over men in the church (1 Ti 2:12), based on the Genesis scripture. Thus, male leadership is not merely a product of Jewish thought; it is God's will for all races and peoples. He desires men to be leaders and heads of both the home and the church, women's liberation movements notwithstanding.

The Negro race in America has suffered from the lack of male leadership. It suffers still, although in recent years the middle-class black man has made some progress in establishing himself as the head of the home. However, there is still no male image in many Negro homes. Getting black men to assume responsibility is a monumental task, even in the church. And getting black women to be less aggressive and more submissive is like trying to snatch a bone from the jaws of a hungry animal. Emancipation did not help here. Reconstruction became a time of moral destruction and disintegration, and over the century the moral clime of Negro family life has improved slowly indeed.

As the economic situation improved, relatively speaking, some Negro men began assuming their rightful, God-given position of authority in the home. Here the growth of the Negro church helped. Frazier credits the new economic position of the male as a major factor in establishing family life, admitting this gain was consolidated by the moral support of the Negro church.[9] Slowly but surely the headship of the male emerged; since preachers were men in authority, this helped to create within the community a better black-male image. A close relationship still existed between family-life organization and church organization. Loose, immoral sex and broken-family behavior are not changed overnight, but the Negro church played a major role in improving the sex behavior of its members.

CRIME

Whites often lament over the "almost complete silence of Negro leaders, including church leaders about 'Negro crime and immorality.' "[10] But whites have not been listening in the right places. Furthermore, until recent years, voices raised within black communities were given no hearing outside those communities.

The rise of "Negro crime" should come as no surprise. Under a strict slavery system there was hardly any crime.[11] White policemen were used primarily to keep track of Negro slave runaways. With emancipation came the inevitable increase in crime, and Southern courts teamed up with the police in using their power and authority to reenslave the black man. Guilt became a matter of color instead of crime committed. Negroes looked upon the police as instruments of injustice and oppression, and upon their fellow blacks, who were convicted by white officials, as victims and martyrs. DuBois points out a curious twofold effect of the appearance of "Negro crime": (1) Negroes refused to believe either the evidence of the whites or their fairness; (2) the whites, used to carelessness so far as justice for Negroes was concerned, swept in moments of murderous passion beyond human decency, reason, democracy, law or order.[12] The vile lynchings and the hellish activities of the white-robed KKKs of yesteryear, coupled with the heinous church bombings and assassinations of today, lend support to the Negroes' opinions.

Concerning the Ku Klux Klan, Booker T. Washington said, "Their objects, in the main, were to crush out the political aspirations of the Negroes, but they did not confine themselves to this, because schoolhouses as well as churches were burned by them, and many innocent persons were made to suffer."[13] Thus the attitudes some Negroes express toward those in authority are understandable. And it must be admitted that white authorities are themselves responsible to some degree for the development of unwholesome attitudes. Even black policemen have not escaped this antagonism from blacks.

Any sincere discussion of "Negro crime" must also include consideration of slums, poverty, crowded housing, ignorance, bigotry, discrimination, unemployment, lack of education, hatred, racism, police brutality, inflated statistics, unequal treatment, corrupt judges and magistrates, and lack of legal aid. All of these things are products of man's sinful heart which is ever ready to manifest its nature under ripe conditions, stimuli, and motivations. Failure to consider the background and history of the black man at this point is unfair, and any discussion of "Negro crime" without this consideration will fall short of accomplishing any good purpose.

CRIME IS AN EXPRESSION OF THE SINFUL HEART

Many factors in life help to determine the way in which the evil in our hearts will express or manifest itself: culture, education, mores, religion, environment, economics, etc. Whether men are civilized or savage, educated or illiterate, living in the suburbs or slums, sin will come out. Statistics, which cannot be fully trusted in this area, show disproportionate numbers of Negroes being arrested and imprisoned, usually for certain crimes such as drunkenness, rape, assault and battery, petty larceny, and murder. However, whites are actually arrested in greater numbers for certain crimes. If more blacks are given the opportunity, we will soon catch up in numbers with the whites who embezzle, defraud, bribe, swindle, commit treason, bomb churches, and commit mass murder. Until recently bank robbery was on this list, but there has been a dramatic increase in the number of Negro bank robbers. This formerly was the white man's "thing" exclusively.

The Mafia and crime syndicates with their dope traffic, lotteries, gambling dens, and prostitution, were neither organized nor ruled by blacks. For that matter, neither did blacks start the last two world wars in which millions of human beings lost their lives. Conservative Christians, fond of stressing the depravity of the human heart, sometimes give the impression that the Negro's heart is more depraved than the heart of other men. It's as if they paraphrase Romans

3:23 as "All have sinned and are falling short of God's glory—especially blacks."

Doubtless, some crimes committed against whites are partially motivated by racial hatred. In June, 1968, three Negroes held up a travel agency in one of our large cities, and one of the robbers told a victim that the holdup was the "white man's fault for the way he had treated my people." The thief made the comment as he took two diamond rings from the finger of a forty-year-old white woman, "It's all the white man's fault. He's making me do this." What a pity that some blacks actually believe this! Some justify criminal acts by directing the spotlight on the oppression, exploitation, fraud, and deceit practiced by some whites. They feel they are right in taking back something long due to them or that which had been stolen from them anyway by the white man. To the natural viciousness of the unregenerate heart is added the motive of revenge. Yet, interestingly, most of the victims of "Negro crime" are themselves black. The main cause of death among Negro men between the ages of fifteen and thirty is murder. And nearly 95 percent of the murderers are black. Representative Raymond Ewell, himself a black man, correctly said while voting against the proposed moratorium on capital punishment in the state of Illinois: "I realize that most of those who would face the death penalty are poor and black and friendless. I also realize that most of their victims are poor and black and friendless and dead!"

EDUCATION

Of course other areas of life were affected by the growth of the church during this period. Mutual-aid societies grew out of the church. Assistance in time of sickness and distress, help for widows and orphans, homes for the aged, handicraft clubs, and schools for domestic training were some of the types of mutual aid offered. The segregated society forced Negroes into these self-help organizations. Participation in American society was severely restricted, especially when Reconstruction ended, so the church filled the gap. One can but dimly imagine the crude concepts of religion and morality, and the ignorance of the more than 4 million poor Negroes emerging from slavery. Booker T. Washington said,

During the whole of the Reconstruction period our people throughout the South looked to the Federal Government for everything, very much as a child looks to its mother. This was not unnatural. The central government gave them freedom, and the whole Nation had been enriched for more than two centuries by the labor of the Negro. Even as a youth, and later in manhood, I had the feeling that it was cruelly wrong in the central government, at the beginning of our freedom, to fail to make some provision for the general education of our people in addition to what the States might do, so that the people would be better prepared for the duties of citizenship.[14]

With freedom, the Negro was left with little means for education. Fortunately, though white Protestants ceased to evangelize the masses of blacks, some turned to the work of educating them. At great personal sacrifice, Northern white men and women came from established churches to set up schools and teach the freed Negroes. Many Negro schools still in existence today were founded during this era of unparalleled educational "missionary" activity.[15] Much of the Negro leadership was provided in this way. Black churches were interested too in the educational development of their people and, in spite of their meager resources, they also set up schools.

Through the church came social cohesion, self-expression, recognition, and leadership. Self-respect and pride were stimulated and preserved, and education was promoted. As nothing else, the church became the Negro's very own. It was the most powerful organization of the black man in America. Said Du Bois,

> . . . a little investigation reveals the curious fact that, in the South, at least, practically every American Negro is a church member. Some, to be sure, are not regularly enrolled, and a few do not habitually attend services; but, practically, a proscribed people must have a social center, and that center for this people is the Negro church. The census of 1890 showed nearly 24,000 Negro churches in this country, with a total enrolled membership of over two and a half millions, or ten actual church members to every 28 persons, and in some Southern States one in every two persons. Besides these there is the large number who, while not enrolled as members, attend and take part in many of the activities of the church.

There is an organized Negro church for every 60 black families in the nation, and in some States for every 40 families, owning, on an average, a thousand dollars' worth of property each, or nearly 26 million dollars in all.[16]

The Negro church also became an arena of political activity. Frazier suggests this came about because Negroes were eliminated from secular politics. Only in the church—on local, associational or denominational levels—could black men hope to become leaders. Outside the church there was little opportunity for the black male to exercise authority, quench the thirst for power, or play the role of a man, as called for by American society.[17]

Methodist ministers in their denominational hierarchies and Baptist preachers in their autonomous local assemblies ruled as monarchs on thrones. The people took great pride in their church meetings in voting for church officers or electing delegates to the various conventions and associational meetings. Unable to vote even for dogcatcher in the outside world, the white man's world, they were serious about every opportunity within the church to participate in expressing their choice and making known their will.

Though their resources were meager, when they pooled their money the church collections were considerable. Control of the church's finances and business activities added to the motivation and resourcefulness of the church politician. Functions which normally belonged to other institutions were assumed by the church. This gave a somewhat religious flavor to the Negro's outlook on life, causing many to observe that the Negro is a very religious being. Though that assumption is false, it is important to remember the church's influence. Usually Negroes did not have to work on Sunday; it was a time of coming together to talk, gossip, have fellowship, flirt, court, eat, and sing. For many, it was an all-day affair. It served as an emotional outlet, a spiritual catharsis, a cause for solidarity, and social cohesion, plus the fact that the gospel was preached and believed and people were saved. Preaching was basically topical and oratorical, not doctrinal and expository. Overemphasis on one type of preaching has resulted in the Negro church being in need of strong doctrinal preaching and teaching, something rarely found in today's average Negro Baptist or Methodist church.

Like any oppressed or enslaved people, Negroes were especially interested in the stories of the Bible which dealt with deliverance and freedom—the Israelites from Egypt, the three Hebrew boys from the fiery furnace, Daniel from the lions' den, heaven and a better life to come. Emancipation did not change this emphasis. There was biblical literalism of the first order. Though many today reject the Scriptures and ridicule the faith of their illiterate forefathers, by that same Word and their faith in Christ, many slaves were saved and went to glory. Remembering that the Negro's heritage is deeply rooted in the church, it should come as no surprise that today much of the social action and civil rights' activities are led by ministers and supported by church members.

5

RADICALISM: 1915-1953

NEGRO POPULATION SHIFTS

Migration to the cities was inevitable. Many Negroes went to the urban centers of the South after the Civil War, but it took the First World War to cause mass migration to Northern cities. This urbanization had a tremendous effect upon the life of the black man. Prior to the war, 90 percent of the Negroes in America lived in the South and most of these, some 80 percent, were in rural areas. When the war came the population began to shift and Negroes headed North. Many reasons were given for the migration: human oppression, forced labor, the Ku Klux Klan, lynchings, etc.

> One hundred Negroes were lynched during the first year of the twentieth century. By the outbreak of the First World War in 1914, the number stood at 1,110. When the war was over, the practice was resumed—28 Negroes being burned alive between 1918 and 1921. Scores of others were hanged, dragged behind automobiles, shot, drowned, or hacked to death.[1]

Natural calamities (boll weevils, floods, etc.) also caused some to leave the South. Northern industry's need for unskilled workers probably played the most important part in drawing the blacks North. The war brought European immigration practically to a halt; from 1914 to 1915 the number of white immigrants decreased from 1,218,480 to 326,700. The cities' black populations increased by leaps and bounds. Today about two-thirds of the black population are city dwellers.

Migration from the farm to the city and from the South to the North brought many difficulties. In housing, there were

48

restrictive covenants, segregation ordinances, and white land-lord exploitation, all of which led to ghettos and the poor health and high mortality that accompany large families liv-ing in small, unsanitary homes. The city's impersonalness and destruction of family life, with increased desertion, ille-gitimacy, and juvenile delinquency, aggravated matters. In-creased migration North created hostility there. Obviously the churches were greatly affected.

DENOMINATIONAL LOYALTY: STATISTICS

Not surprisingly, the migrants generally continued their denominational affiliations. Those who were Baptists in the South were still Baptists in the North. The Methodists also remained relatively loyal to their denomination. Statistics in 1916 for the four major all-black groups were: Baptists, 3,196,623; AME, 545,814; AMEZ, 456,813; CME, 202, 713.

The 1971 World Almanac gives this breakdown for 1970: National Baptist Convention, USA, Inc., 6,487,003; National Baptist Convention of America, 2,668,799; Progressive Bap-tist Convention 521,692; AME, 1,166,301; AMEZ, 850, 389; and CME, 466,718.

These statistics do not tell the complete story, of course. Pentecostal and apostolic churches are omitted; figures for some groups are difficult to obtain.

Today nearly one million Negroes are in the major white churches. Latest figures available are found in the Negro Handbook of 1966. They are: Methodist Episcopal, 373, 327; American Baptist, 200,000. There may be some over-lap here because some National Baptist churches are dually aligned, belonging both to the Negro conventions and to the white convention. They are listed as follows: Congregational, 38,000; Christian Churches (Disciples of Christ), 80,000; Protestant Episcopal, 73,867; Seventh Day Adventist, 167, 892; United Church of Christ, 21,859; United Presbyterian, USA, 6,000. Add to these the nearly 800,000 black Roman Catholics and the many other smaller Protestant groups and we estimate there are two million Negroes belonging to pre-dominantly white denominations, compared with the esti-mated twelve million belonging to black denominations.

BAPTISTS

One characteristic of Baptists is the tendency to split. With no other outlets for politicking, the church became the political arena, and the mad scramble for leadership and control led to splits, withdrawals, and reorganizations, creating a host of "New" and "Greater" Baptist churches. This explains the Peace and Rest Baptist Church on one corner, and the Greater Peace and Rest Baptist Church on another corner of the same block. When the National Baptist Convention split in 1915, the cause was more than "the legal entanglements over the adoption of a charter and the exclusive ownership of a publishing house." Joseph Washington states:

> This legal explosion of Negro Baptists into two groups with identical eccelesiastical nomenclature and social motivation can be accounted for in large measure by external socio-economic pressures. With no higher loyalty than to the race and its progress, and with little or no success in advancing against the seemingly invulnerable common enemy, Negro Baptists turned their wrath and hostility inward upon themselves. The only channel at the disposal of the Negro for implosion was religion.

> Baptists, constituting the vast majority of Negroes, were accustomed to local autonomy, and their congregations provided the perfect medium for the free airing of personal disappointments, discontent and disillusionment. Dashed hopes, feuds, factions, and fights created Negro politicians. In this atmosphere of tension, the Baptist preacher arose as the master politician who continued as the leader of the people by diverting them from their external failures in society through practical politics in a religious setting.

> Since 1915, the heavy concentration of Negroes in the South has been largely denied the privilege of political expression. The local congregation has filled this need and has created through city, county, state, and national Baptist associations a political outlet for the Negro. The explosion which created two national conventions continued down through county, state, city and local bodies. . . . On the local level, this division of Baptists persists, partly because the external forces have not substantially changed and partly because splits are the habitual way of Negro Baptists.[2]

Secularization of the Churches

One thing is sure: the Negro churches in the North were not prepared for the great influx that took place during and after World War I. The result: new sects and storefront churches came into existence, and what Frazier calls the secularization of the churches began.[3] Secularization drew the Negro away from a religious orientation to a worldly one where the temporal was stressed rather than the spiritual.

Otherworldliness was a major characteristic of the emphasis of the Negro church during slavery and until the end of the nineteenth century. But things formerly opposed—such as jazz, drinking, dancing, card-playing, and theater-going— were no longer regarded as sinful by all the churchgoers. Significantly, this "secularization" trend was countered in some measure by the birth of church groups stressing "holiness." In addition to an increased tolerance of things formerly considered wrong or immoral, there was a growing concern for the here and now. More Negro ministers began to dabble in politics. And more interest was expressed in community affairs.

Church ministers and members became more interested in self-help and racial-advancement organizations such as the NAACP (National Association for the Advancement of Colored People), and the Urban League. They expressed their interest with membership drives, financial contributions, special sermons, and the availability of the church building for meetings.

The Storefront Church

With secularization came the storefront church. Certain psychological, social, and economic reasons created more black churches, proportionately, than white. "Overchurching" seems to have political origins, although many men claim definite leading of the Holy Spirit to form and organize such assemblies. A storefront, as the name implies, is generally a church conducted in an unrented or abandoned store. Sometimes it is a housefront church; this is a home or private residence converted into a church, often to the dismay of the second-floor occupants or the adjoining homeowners.

While the majority of storefront churches are Baptist, many are cults or sects, or Apostolic, Holiness, or Pentecostal groups; few are affiliated with the Methodists. These churches exist because the Southern migrant attempts to reestablish a little bit of home, to cling to the traditional way of worship and type of preaching. The impersonal big cities have lost their sense of "peopleness"; members are just envelope numbers or dues-payers. Storefronts offer identification, belonging, acceptance, recognition, all lacking in large depersonalized congregations. Emotional and economic needs and educational levels are important considerations also, as is the matter of status of whether one is a Northerner or Southerner.

Perhaps the main reason for beginning storefronts was that the established Southern churches did not follow up their members who left. Then, too, the failure of established Northern churches to contact, welcome, and win these newcomers, has a bearing on the number of such assemblies found in urban areas. However, Preston Williams points out,

> They had left the soil and life of their ancestors and come to the wonderful world of the northern city where freedom and opportunities were said to exist. But they found neither freedom nor opportunity. They were robbed even of personal fellowship and social camaraderie. To believe that the "Black Church" could have successfully met this challenge is to believe in magic, not miracles. To attribute its failure to meet this need to a defective theology or a desire for self-segregation; to the perfidy of its clergy or the power drives of its people is simply to play the role of a fool or White man's jester. The Black Church simply had no way of meeting the crisis of the twenties and thirties. It lacked the theological, financial, educational and other resources that this situation demanded. The theological resources were nowhere present in America.[4]

It is true that some men who organize storefronts do so out of their own vanity and ego and the desire to be leaders. Conflicts of leadership within the established denominations also help increase the number of such churches. But it is also true that some leaders desire to be used by the Lord Jesus Christ to win souls unto Him and nourish those souls in God's Word. There are black preachers who have finished either Bible school or seminary and have been unable to get an audience in churches with vacant pulpits. Sometimes this is due to the evangelical beliefs of these men and their teaching of the separated life, things which keep them out of the cliques to which other ministers belong. The point is, some men have obviously been led of the Spirit of God to found such assemblies. And God has blessed their efforts.

Some Negroes look down their noses at storefronts. Criticism often voiced asks, "Why are there so many of them? Look! Four in one block. Why don't they get together?" And the fact that some of the ministers are poorly trained is often mentioned; they are referred to as "jackleg" preachers. Whatever the motivations and reasons for their existence, and in spite of the criticisms, the storefronts do serve a good purpose. As Frazier remarks, it is irrelevant in a sense and useless to try to answer the question, "Are we overchurched?" For many blacks in the North and South, the storefront still represents a haven from the cruel white world and affords the only true fellowship and social life they have. This is not to overlook the fact that where the Word of God is faithfully preached and taught, sinners are saved and the saved sinners are edified.

CULTS AND THE NEGRO

Some Negroes have repudiated Christianity altogether and have joined radical cults, religious groups regarded as unorthodox because in certain beliefs, interpretations, or practices they differ from other religious groups considered as the standard expressions of religion. Each cult seems to play up some weak point or neglected area of the orthodox denominations. Christian Science stresses divine healing, a matter most denominational churches have shied away from. The so-called "apostolics" stress the deity of Christ, a doctrine seemingly forgotten by some of today's social-gospel activists. The Jehovah's Witnesses emphasize prophecy, something else which many denominational churches avoid. Among other things, Father Divine's movement emphasizes fellowship or integration, and black-white togetherness—something which far too many Evangelicals have great difficulty with.

Each cult takes a truth, blows it out of proportion, mixes in error and falsehood, and deceives the unwary. Undoubtedly the Black Muslims exist because of the failure of many white professing Christians to recognize black Christians as their brothers, or to treat the black man with respect, justice and equality. Many Negroes have become easy prey for the cults. Bahai and Christian Science advertise regularly in the leading Negro newspapers of our large cities. Some intellectual blacks have turned to Unitarianism and ethical societies. Jehovah's Witnesses have made great strides among the blacks because their emphasis on teaching has appealed to the hungry hearts of the doctrine-starved former members of Negro Baptist and Methodist churches. Considering the circumstances, it is no wonder that so many are drawn to these unorthodox groups. Certainly the religious-economic-social background of the American black man lends itself to such aberrations and errors.

Fauset has suggested that the following factors—listed in what he believes is the order of importance—attract members to these cults:[5] (1) personality of the leader, (2) the desire to draw closer to God, (3) racial or nationalistic urge, (4) miraculous healing, (5) dissatisfaction with Christianity as it is known, (6) a disdain for orthodox churches, (7) mental relief afforded by the cult, (8) an urge for leadership and participation, (9) help to one's business, (10) a dislike for the clergy, (11) the fact that the cult teaches, (12) finding within the cult a common bond of friendliness, understanding, and sympathy, elements all too often lacking in more orthodox assemblies.

WHY THE CULTS?

As mentioned, Jehovah's Witnesses' success in teaching is largely due to the fact that souls are hungry and too often they are not fed or taught in black Baptist and Methodist churches. Many times I have spoken to Witnesses who said they never learned anything as Baptists. One lady Witness, who had been a Sunday school teacher for twenty-five years in a large Baptist church, told me she had never heard of the Battle of Armageddon until she joined the Witnesses. This is not surprising because her former pastor once declared that the book of Revelation was so full of symbolism and so controversial that he had no intention of ever preaching from it.

Cults teach their people and challenge their minds; doctrine is foremost. But it is also true that some cults are strong because they stress the supernatural: faith-healing, speaking in tongues, and tarrying for the Holy Spirit and a second blessing, etc. Some cults as well as the Christian groups came into being because of the glaring inconsistencies of the established churches. Groups which stress "holiness" exist in part as protests against the carnality and wickedness of orthodox denominational church members and leaders. Some blacks have found greater acceptance in "white" cults than in conservative assemblies. A black man can attend the Watchtower Society's Gideon School but he cannot attend nor is he welcome at certain fundamentalist institutions in America. Thus, the need for fellowship and the sense of belonging are supplied by the cults, fulfillments often not found in the denominational churches.

Admittedly, some cults are racial, so their appeal is due to racial identification and the provision of a refuge from the white man's cruel world and impersonal city life. After analyzing all the reasons why blacks are attracted to the cults, as well as the personalities of the founders and leaders, the economic, social, and spiritual conditions of their members, and their need to fulfill their desire of being wanted and loved and the feeling of belonging, plus the faults and failures of the orthodox and established churches, there still remains the matter of the sin of unbelief in the human heart.

And there is the role played by Satan, the world's greatest deceiver and the father of every cult, false belief, and "ism." Sociologists with their facts and figures fail to recognize this malignant being who directs all cult activity. But Bible-centered believers cannot afford to gloss over Satan's work in this area. We know that the world is asleep in Satan's lap, but we rejoice because Christ who is in us is greater than the devil in the world.

Three main cults which were begun during this Radicalism period of 1915-53 were the Apostolics, Father Divine, and the Black Muslims. Each group will be considered separately.

THE APOSTOLICS

Perhaps the largest and best known of the Apostolics is the Church of the Lord Jesus Christ of the Apostolic Faith, founded by the late Bishop Sherrod C. Johnson. Born in Halifax County, North Carolina, in 1898, Johnson went to Philadelphia before he was twenty to become a businessman.

He met several holiness preachers in North Philadelphia and shortly afterward, according to a church spokesman, differed with them and started preaching in his home. As the number of his followers grew, they moved three times to larger quarters. In October 1947 the church purchased the building of the Bethany Collegiate Presbyterian Church for $105,000. Founded in 1858 by John Wanamaker, who was superintendent of its Sunday school until his death in 1922, it was considered one of the largest Presbyterian churches in the world. The building burned to the ground in November, 1958. Betty Ann McDowell, ten years old, one of about 1,500 worshipers when the seven-alarm blaze was discovered, died in the building. Bishop Johnson immediately set out to build a one-story structure with a seating capacity of 3,500. The basement chapel can accommodate 1,500 and there are offices, a dining hall, a nursery, and a studio room for broadcasts. The building was constructed with a minimum of paid labor, for workmen and laborers who were church members contributed hours of work. Bishop Johnson insisted that the building proceed on a pay-as-you-go basis. There were no mortgages, no indebtedness, and no public solicitation of funds, although estimates of the value of the structure range to one million dollars.

In January, 1961, Bishop Johnson arrived in Kingston, Jamaica, to visit a branch of his church. Addressing a large meeting on February 17, the bishop collapsed. He was taken to the home of an elder, where he died of pneumonia. In conformity with the tenet of his church, there was no viewing and no formal funeral.

For more than twenty years Bishop Johnson broadcast in Philadelphia. In time, his talks were taped and sent out over more than sixty other radio stations. More than ninety congregations, including three in the West Indies and one at Toronto, Canada, have sprung from the original church. Communicants number many thousands. Today the organization is headed by Bishop S. McDowell Shelton.

Under the late Bishop Johnson the organization practiced washing of feet and prohibited the wearing of cosmetics and silk stockings, straightening of hair, using alcoholic beverages, and attending the movie theater. Members were forbidden to watch television or listen to the radio except to hear the bishop. He was also against women preachers. However, other Apostolic assemblies are not as stringent.

Bishop Johnson claimed that (1) he was an apostle; (2) Christ is no longer the Son of God; (3) you must speak in tongues in order to be saved; (4) Acts 2:38 is the key verse in the Bible; (5) there is no Trinity; (6) the words, "I baptize you in the name of Jesus Christ," must be pronounced over the candidate or else he is not saved; and (7) Jesus Christ *is* the Father (the Father's name is Jesus)!

This so-called Apostolic Church movement is an indication of the apostasy predicted in 2 Peter and Jude. In answer to Bishop Johnson's seven claims are the following biblical truths:

1. There are no apostles today, and the true apostolic church ceased with the death of John the apostle in about 100 A.D.

2. Christ's sonship is not based upon the incarnation; He did not *become* the Son at birth or give up His sonship at death. Jesus Christ always was, is now, and ever shall be the Son of God.

> We meet certain professed Christians today who deny what is called the Eternal Sonship of Christ. They tell us He was not Son from eternity. They admit He was the Word, as set forth in John 1:1, but they say He became the Son when He was born on earth. Galatians 4:4 definitely denies any such teaching. "God sent forth His Son to be born of a woman." He was the Son before He ever stooped from the heights of glory to the virgin womb. It was the Son who came in grace to become Man in order that we might be saved.
>
> This same truth is set forth in 1 John 4:9, 10: "In this was manifested the love of God toward us, because God sent His only begotten Son into the world that we might live through Him. Herein is love, not that we loved God, but that He loved us, and sent His Son to be the propitiation for our sins." Nothing could be clearer than the two definite statements in these verses. God sent His Son, sent Him into the world, sent Him from heaven, even as John 3:16 declares. We dishonor the Lord Jesus Christ if we deny His eternal Sonship. If He be not the Eternal Son, then God is not the Eternal Father.[6]

3. Speaking in tongues is not essential to salvation.

4. Acts 2:38 is not the key verse of the Bible. The book of Acts is a historical account of the birth and growth of the church; it is a record of a time of change, transition and development.

> In our century, there are those who try to tell us that the church should be today just as it was in the book of the Acts. I thank God that this is not true. The church of the book of the Acts was a church without a New Testament. The church at the end of the apostolic age was a church that possessed the New Testament. There is a vast difference between the two. The church of the year following Pentecost was a church of tongues and imitation tongues, of signs and false signs, of movements of the Spirit and of counterfeits of such movements. This we know from a close study of the letters to Thessalonica and Corinth.[7]

5. The Bible definitely teaches that the one true and living God exists as Father, Son and Holy Spirit at the same time.

6. What is said over a candidate for baptism is a formula nowhere given in the Bible, nor does salvation depend upon such a formula.

7. Jesus Christ is not God the Father, but God the Son who came to make known the Father to all mankind (Jn 1:18). No man has or can see God as He fully and essentially exists—as Father, Son, and Holy Spirit. God absolute is more than God revealed.

FATHER DIVINE

LEARNING TO BE GOD

Joseph Washington considers the Father Divine Peace Mission Movement as a combination "faith-healing" and "holiness" cult. Frazier also states that the movement is the most important and most widely known of the holiness cults.[8] The "holiness" is seen in the group's tenets which include no undue mixing of the sexes, no smoking, drinking, dancing, vulgarity, profanity or obscenity, and no receiving of gifts, presents, tips, or bribes.

Who was Father Divine? George Baker—that was his name before he became "God"—was born on a plantation to sharecropper parents in about 1865 on Hutchinson Island on the Savannah River, Georgia. In 1899 he met the Reverend

St. John the Divine Hickerson, a dynamic Negro mystic, in Baltimore, Maryland, where Hickerson pastored a Baptist church. Baker met another Negro preacher of great personal magnetism or charisma, Samuel Morris, who somehow convinced Baker that since God dwelt in him, he *was* God and so entitled to divine authority; he said this was according to the scriptures, 1 Corinthians 3:16 and 6:19.

Baker and Morris teamed up; then Hickerson joined them in 1908. The trio continued until 1912 when dissension split their ranks. The dispute centered on who was really deity and who was not. Baker then headed back South, preaching that *he* was "God." He was arrested in Valdosta, Georgia, in 1914. When he refused to give his name, the court writ read: "The people vs. John Doe, Alias God." Found guilty as a community menace, he was run out of town.

In 1915 he arrived in New York City with some of his followers and once more he contacted Hickerson, and again became a student of the art of being "God." Shortly after coming to New York, he married a girl named Penninah, one of his faithful followers from Valdosta, Georgia. However, J. Austin Norris, Father Divine's attorney, states that Father actually married Penninah on June 6, 1882. In 1941 Penninah disappeared from public view and only after he had married a second time in 1946 did he admit to his followers that his first wife had died.

DIVINE RETRIBUTION

In 1919 his church had nearly two dozen members. Needing more space, he bought a two-story frame house for $2,500 in the all-white community of Sayville, Long Island. Then he opened a free employment bureau and soon began to take in the poor and needy and feed them. He was then known as Major Devine, but a few years later he changed the spelling to Divine. The white neighbors thought it was bad enough having Negroes in the neighborhood, but when busloads of blacks came from Harlem every weekend to eat fried chicken, pork chops, salad, vegetables, and dessert (it was during the Depression) they began complaining. The loud all-night singing and chanting of Father's followers and the fact that women were living in the house were reported to the authorities.

On November 15, 1931, the house was raided on the charge of disturbing the peace. Father's bail was canceled and

he was jailed as a public nuisance during the trial. Eighty of
his members were also arrested. The judge, State Supreme
Court Justice, Lewis J. Smith, having no respect for Father's
deity, sentenced Father Divine to one year in jail and fined
him $500. Smith, a Presbyterian, was disgusted to hear edu-
cated white men and women testify that Father Divine was
God personified. This sentencing occurred on May 24, 1932.
Four days later, Judge Smith, apparently having been in excellent health, dropped dead of a heart attack. He was fifty
years old. Father Divine was told about it while in jail, and is
quoted to have said, "I hated to do it." Needless to say, this
was the shot in the arm used by Satan to spur on the movement.

WEALTH OF THE MOVEMENT

After this "divine retribution," the conviction was reversed
and Father Divine was freed on June 24, 1932. From that
point on, money poured in, until today the movement is worth
an estimated twenty million dollars. Their attorney says there
is no shortage of funds; he estimates their holdings in Pennsylvania, New Jersey, and New York at approximately twelve
million dollars. Interestingly, the organization's more sub-
stantial financial support has come from white people.

The United States government has not figured out the source
of Father Divine's income. Since he claims to be deity, he is
supposed to own everything in the whole world. Evidently he
does not claim ownership of the New Jersey Turnpike, for
his followers are forbidden to travel on it. Father was fined
$60 in 1953 for speeding on the turnpike.

IMMORALITY

Ruth Boaz, a white woman who left the movement and
became a Christian, wrote an article revealing Father Divine
as "a charlatan, a false god, cruel and cynical impostor . . .
the Devil incarnate."[9] Miss Boaz admitted having sexual relations with Father Divine, who evidently freely engaged in
adultery while preaching sexual abstinence or "non-sex," as he
called it, to his followers. Even married couples who joined
the movement were separated and not allowed to live together. Yet Father Divine indulged in sex. When asked why by
Miss Boaz, he replied that "God" does as he pleases, and that

he sought to eliminate her desire by bringing it to the surface. This blasphemer who called himself "God" was exposed some years earlier in the 1930s by one Viola Wilson or Faithful Mary, who told substantially the same thing about Father Divine's sex life.[10]

In 1946 Father Divine married Edna Rose Ritchings, a white Canadian then known as Sweet Angel, now as Mother Divine. She was twenty-one; Father was eighty or eighty-one. The ceremony was performed by a Baptist minister in Washington, D.C. Mother Divine is now head of the movement, controlling the money and making the important decisions. It is noteworthy that, according to Miss Boaz, four of the six top officials in the movement now are white.

THE DEATH OF GOD

Father Divine died on September 10, 1965, leaving behind a million deluded followers. Mother Divine, pointing out that his death involved only the physical body, said, "Like Jesus, although his body is gone, he is still with us." Much praise from various sources was given Father Divine upon his death. The Philadelphia *Inquirer* headlined: "Negro Leaders Grieve at Father Divine's Death." The article said,

> Leaders of the Philadelphia Negro community expressed grief at the death of Father Divine on Friday and offered praise for the influence the Negro evangelist exerted on his followers. "I was deeply grieved to learn of his passing," said the Rev. Leon H. Sullivan, founder of the O.I.C. and pastor of the Zion Baptist Church. ". . . In my opinion, he was the forerunner . . . of much that we see in the practical aspects of religion today. While many people were yet talking about what religion could do about integration and self-determination and human dignity, he was practicing it."
>
> Father Divine was called a "force for good and stability in the community" by U.S. Representative Robert N. C. Nix (D., Phila.). Nix said Father Divine's followers "were taught a high degree of morality . . . paid their bills . . . were good constructive citizens." . . .
>
> Father Divine's death was described as a "great loss," by Cecil B. Moore, president of the Philadelphia branch of the NAACP. "We think he lived and demonstrated by his life, principles we are fighting for."[11]

The Philadelphia *Evening Bulletin* said in an editorial that the movement

> has achieved what many more formally organized denominations cry for—that the followers give up all that they have and commit themselves to the faith without stint.
>
> The cult has been, too, especially in its earlier days in the Depression, a sort of private war on poverty. It lifted people out of poverty, got them higher wages, gave them country estates. . . . A New York alderman in 1939 estimated that Father Divine was saving the city 2 million dollars a year in relief payments alone. . . . The honesty, obedience to law and diligence of his followers became a trade mark. And long before racial integration became a national issue he made it seem as natural and innocent as the life in Eden. . . . The Philadelphia area has lost one of its most memorable men.[12]

The organization's attorney said, "No matter what anybody says, he has done a lot of good. A lot of good." To this Walter Martin replies,

> One of the most common objections raised by many erstwhile do-gooders, who are almost totally ignorant of Biblical theology, is that Father Divine, while certainly in error, or mentally unbalanced regarding his obsession of his "deity," has apparently done many wonderful works for others. Therefore these persons maintain that he is doing, in a sense, the works of God, ignorant though he may be of their origin and operation.
>
> To this apparently reasonable objection the Scriptures offer a complete refutation, for it was the Lord Jesus Himself who, when asked by the Jews, "What shall we do, that we might work the works of God?" (John 6:28), replied, "This is the work of God, that you believe on him whom he hath sent" (verse 29). All of Father Divine's good works are not *the* work of God, which is believing in and living for Jesus Christ as Savior and Lord. This work in turn results in works that *God* reckons good, because they are done through Him, and not through the selfish motive of self-justification or personal glory.[13]

A SOCIAL GOSPELER'S LACK OF SPIRITUAL DISCERNMENT

On September 28, 1968, on the Woodmont estate, Gladwyne, Pennsylvania, Father Divine's mausoleum shrine, costing between $250,000 and $300,000, was dedicated. The aforementioned nationally known Negro minister, Leon H. Sullivan, said,

> Peace Father, Peace Mother, Peace everyone: I want all of you to know how moved I have been and how moved I am now. It is truly wonderful. And to see how the Spirit of Father yet abounds in our midst and in the world! . . . when first I came to Philadelphia . . . one of the first wonderful and glorious experiences I had was when I had the great Privilege and Honor of being in the presence of Father . . . whenever I was faced with problems of perplexity, and wanted to try to do something to help my community, I would seek an appointment and council with Father.
>
> I think there is nothing that I have been involved with try- ing to do that Father did not know about—and I would come to Father and . . . I would talk about something I'd want to do and I would ask Him about it, and then I would say, "Well, now will you help me?" and he would say, "Yes, I will help you."
>
> And there was never a meeting, a public meeting that I held, that I did not always somehow reach Father to ask him to pray for its success. I will never forget him. He will always be with me like he is with you. In my labors and in my work as I strive to bring Peace, alleviate poverty and help to eradi- cate prejudice, I should want Father to know, and you, Mother, to know, that wherever I go the Spirit of Father is in and with me—and I want you to know that if any success comes to my work, I want you to know, and I mean this pro- foundly—that if any success comes to my work, that Father is in that success too! Peace! Peace Everyone!"[14]

Such blasphemy indicates the delusion of the age in which we live. Walter Martin closes the case against Father Divine:

> Father Divine, or George Baker, has irrevocably com- mitted the sin of blasphemy against the only true God. More- over, he has claimed to be what his own soul knows he is not, and it is as certain as the rising of the sun that he must some day answer for the terrible delusions he has foisted on the minds of over a million persons.[15]

THE BLACK MUSLIMS

"BLACK" PREFERRED

Personally, I have no hangups about what you call me or the members of my race. It is said that "colored" is passé, and used only by the older generation. "African" was the title preferred by the first freed slaves in this country. "Afro-American" never really caught on and is considered too unwieldy. "Negro," which means black in Spanish, is now considered Establishment by the militants; supposedly it is used only by the over-thirty age group. Some whites still offend with their lower case "negro." Whether used as a noun or an adjective, Negro should be capitalized. So what is left? "Black." Formerly a descriptive adjective of contempt, today its use as a noun and adjective is preferred, almost demanded, by the under-thirty age group.[16]

I recall that at one Black Muslim meeting, the minister said, "Everybody here who's proud he's black, stand up!" Every Muslim, would-be Muslim, and sympathizer jumped up like quail taking off in a field. I remained seated. The minister then fixed his eyes upon me and, with scorn in his voice, asked me if I wanted to be white. I sat there. Then he proceeded to call out different colors, including "technicolor," to see which one I would be proud to own, which one would bring me to my feet. I thought to myself: *How ridiculous! God made me the color I am. Is skin color something to be proud of? Or ashamed of? If I'm proud I'm black, does it mean the Caucasian is to be pitied and despised because his skin is white?* Needless to say, because of my defiant attitude I was politely but firmly asked to leave the mosque.

One phenomenon on the current racial scene in America is the attempt by some Negroes to escape their traditional lowly status by preaching the superiority of the black man. And make no mistake about it, the Black Muslims believe they are superior. Some Negroes teach that the first inhabitants of this earth were black, and that true Israelites are black, implying that white-skin Jews are frauds. Some Negroes teach that Jesus Christ was a black man; others teach that God Himself is black! We are told that to know Christ was a black man will make other black men realize they play a more important role in the world than they are credited for generally. The idea seems to be that if black men knew such "truths" they would be set free from the shackles of an inferiority complex.

THE MOORISH SCIENCE TEMPLE

The Black Muslim cult is not the first group to make such a radical departure from the traditional black religion. The Moorish Science Temple of America was perhaps the immediate predecessor of the Black Muslims. This cult was founded by Timothy Drew, a Negro born in North Carolina in 1886. He became obsessed with the idea that the salvation of the black man was to be found in the discovery of his national origin. He taught that we should no longer be called Negroes, black folk, colored people, or Ethiopians. Obviously, recent debate about what name to use is really nothing new. Drew said that the words *Negro* or *black* symbolize death; "colored" means painted. And since we are neither dead nor painted, the term that suits us best is "Moorish-American."

Drew had, as all of these cult leaders possess, a certain personal magnetism. His apparent sincere desire to help his people escape race prejudice and discrimination proved valuable in his efforts to establish temples. He started in Newark, New Jersey, in 1913 and became known as Noble Drew Ali. The cult professed to honor all divine prophets: Jesus, Muhammad, Buddha, Confucius, Zoroaster, and others. Preaching that a change in identification (Negro to Asiatic) would bring salvation, hundreds in Chicago (which became the center of the organization) joined him. Membership may have been as high as twenty or thirty thousand during the lifetime of the "Prophet."[17]

In time, internal strife erupted; a leader, Sheik Claude Greene, was killed. Arrested for murder, Noble Drew Ali died under mysterious circumstances in 1929 while released on bond and waiting for trial. After Ali's death the cult split into a number of factions. The leader of one of the surviving splinter groups was none other than Wallace D. Fard or Farrad Mohammad or Wali Farrad, who initially considered himself the "reincarnation of Ali." Fard, who was later proclaimed to have been "Allah in Person," was once a peddler of "exotic goods" (silk, incense, perfumes, etc.) in the Negro sections of the city of Detroit. Some say that he was a white man, which of course, if true, would be an embarrassment to the Black Muslims. Others describe him as being of "light color" with "an Oriental cast of countenance." All this is difficult to ascertain since so much mystery surrounds Fard.

MR. MUHAMMAD

The man who later became Mr. Muhammad came to Detroit in 1923 with his wife and two children. He heard Fard
speak in 1930 and was impressed by his preaching that the
white man was a devil. Converted, Muhammad joined Fard.
Although Muhammad had only an eighth-grade education,
his organizational ability was quickly recognized and he
rose to become Fard's chief minister. Fard vanished in 1934
and it is reported that Mr. Muhammad, now the "last Mes-
senger from Allah," was the last to see him. So it was that the
Black Muslims, founded in 1930 by Fard and having made
little headway, came under Mr. Muhammad's leadership. The
organization made little progress under Mr. Muhammad for
many years until the Second World War came.

Who is Mr. Muhammad? He was born Elijah Poole on
October 7, 1897, in Sandersville, Georgia, one of thirteen
children born to Wali and Marie Poole, former slaves. His
father was a poor Baptist preacher. After meeting "Allah on
earth," Poole dropped his "slave master's name" of Poole and
took the spiritual surname, Muhammad. The "X" used by
the Muslims represents their unknown true name, taken away
by the white slave masters centuries earlier.

In April, 1934, Detroit police arrested him, charging him
with contributing to the delinquency of a minor. He had refused to send one of his children to the public school and
was educating him instead at a Muslim parochial school he
had set up. The result: six months' probation. In November
of that year some of his would-be followers, disgusted with
his teaching, drove him out of the city. He settled in Chicago
and made it his permanent headquarters.

When World War II came, he preached against the draft
as the white man's draft for the white man's war. When
the FBI tracked him down in September, 1942, they found
him rolled up in a carpet under a bed in his mother's home in
Chicago. Seventy-one of his followers were arrested on charg-
es of sedition and draft evasion. Muhammad was convicted
and sent to the federal prison at Milan, Michigan, where he
stayed until 1946.

Prisons have proved to be fertile ground for recruitment
for the Black Muslims. While their leaders preach hatred in
the principal cities across America, lesser lights inside prisons

all across the country also spread their doctrines and recruit new "brothers." Said Dr. Lincoln:

> The prisons are made to order for Muhammad. Nine times out of ten, the potential convert was arrested by a white policeman, sentenced by a white judge, directed by a white prison guard under a white warden. The prison chaplain was white, and he knew when he got out that he could not go to a white church for help. The Negro church was not interested, but there was Elijah waiting.[18]

MALCOLM X

One prize prisoner who was converted was Malcolm Little, better known as Malcolm X. Born in Omaha, Nebraska, in 1925, he was the son of a Baptist minister. He spent most of his early life in Lansing, Michigan. "Big Red," as he was known, entered a life of crime and was twice convicted for larceny. During his second incarceration in Concord, Massachusetts, in 1947, he became a Black Muslim. After his release he became the movement's chief spokesman. The Black Muslims' existence was practically unknown to whites and many Negroes. It is significant that E. Franklin Frazier makes no mention of the movement in his book *The Negro Church in America,* although it was published in 1962.

It was in 1958, about thirty-seven years after the cult's birth, that recognition came. On April 14, 1958, squads of the New York City police rushed to Seventh Avenue and 125th Street in Harlem, to break up a fight between two Negro men. One newspaper reported:

> The police engaged in an altercation with Johnson Hinton, a Negro who was not party to the fight, knocked him to the ground, and arrested him. It might have been a commonplace incident if Hinton had not been a Black Muslim and a mem- of Malcolm X's temple. A huge crowd of angry Negroes, estimated at more than 500 by police, immediately threw a cordon around the local police station. Officials grew alarmed and were happy to contact Malcolm X when they were advised to do so by a Negro newspaperman.

> Upon his arrival at the police station, Malcolm demanded that Hinton be removed to a hospital. This was done and, at a signal from Malcolm, the crowd quickly and quietly dispersed. Hinton later won a $75,000 damage claim against

the city of New York, and Harlem police marked Malcolm and the Black Muslims as something to keep an eye on. It was after this that Malcolm became widely known as Muhammad's emissary. He crisscrossed the nation, recruiting Negroes and frightening many whites, in one of the most amazingly successful missionary campaigns ever conducted in the U.S.[19]

MALCOLM FALLS INTO DISFAVOR

Malcolm X was silenced by Mr. Muhammad for saying the assassination of President Kennedy was a "case of chickens coming home to roost." This was probably just an excuse to cut down Malcolm. Behind it all may have been jealousy of Malcolm's prestige and influence; perhaps Mr. Muhammad's own children, active in the cult, viewed with alarm Malcolm's growing fame. I. F. Stone, in the article "The Pilgrimage of Malcolm X" gives this appraisal:

> On the one side envy and on the other disillusions were to drive the two men apart. The crowds drawn by Malcolm and his very organizing success made Elijah Muhammad and his family jealous. On the other hand, Malcolm, who had kept the sect's vows of chastity, was shocked when former secretaries of Elijah Muhammad filed paternity suits against the prophet. Malcolm had nothing but a small salary and the house the sect had provided for him.
>
> Elijah Muhammad's cars (two Cadillacs and a Lincoln Continental), his $200 pin-striped banker-styled suits, his elegantly furnished 18-room house in one of the better sections of Chicago's Hyde Park, began to make a sour impression on Malcolm. The hierarchy lives well in practically all religions, and their worldly affluence fosters schism. Malcolm was too big, too smart, too able, to fit into the confines of this little sect and remain submissive to its family oligarchy. He began to open up a larger world, and this endangered Elijah Muhammad's hold on the little band of unsophisticated faithful he had recruited.[20]

Malcolm left the movement in March, 1964, and for five months toured Africa and the Middle East. He attacked Mr. Muhammad as a phony and a racist. The organization splintered badly, many men leaving it altogether. From a peak of perhaps 100,000, the organization is down to perhaps less than 25,000 now. Unfortunately, it is doubtful if many of the defectors have reevaluated their attitude toward Christianity or the white man. Evidently Malcolm had his eyes opened somewhat on the race issue and consequently he sought to establish a "true" Muslim organization with the blessings, he said, of the Muslims of Africa and the Middle East. From Jedda, Saudi Arabia, on April 20, 1964, he wrote:

> You may be shocked by these words coming from me, but I have always been a man who tries to face facts, and to accept the reality of life as new experiences and knowledge unfold it. The experiences of this pilgrimage have taught me much, and each hour here in the Holy Land opens my eyes even more.

When he returned to Chicago he said:

> In the past, I have permitted myself to be used to make sweeping indictments of all white people, and these generalizations have caused injuries to some white people who did not deserve them. Because of the spiritual rebirth which I was blessed to undergo as a result of my pilgrimage to the Holy City of Mecca, I no longer subscribe to sweeping indictments of one race.

> My pilgrimage to Mecca . . . served to convince me that perhaps American whites can be cured of the rampant racism which is consuming them and about to destroy this country. In the future, I intend to be careful not to sentence anyone who has not been proven guilty. I am not a racist and do not subscribe to any of the tenets of racism.

> In all honesty and sincerity it can be stated that I wish nothing but freedom, justice and equality: life, liberty and the pursuit of happiness—for all people. My first concern is with the group of people to which I belong, the Afro-Americans, for we, more than other people, are deprived of these inalienable rights.[21]

Malcolm's violent death came on Sunday, February 21, 1965, when assassins pumped more than a dozen bullets into his body. The murderers, who were later caught, convicted and imprisoned, were said to be former members of the Black Muslims, but Mr. Muhammad steadfastly denied that his organization had anything to do with Malcolm's murder.

Ben Holman wrote that "a survey of the Garveyites, the Moorish Scientists or any of the myriad other minor black supremacy, pseudo-Moslem cults that have flourished among American Negroes would show that Elijah Muhammad, for all his acclaim, has not promulgated one idea not previously advanced." This is true. However, what Mr. Muhammad has put forth is succeeding, and no other similar group has ever accomplished what the Black Muslims have done. Even the fact that the more than 100,000 true Muslims in the United States have expressed their disagreement with Muhammad's deprecation of the white man has not deterred the Muslims. "Most foreign Moslems dispute the contention that Muhammad is a legitimate teacher of Islam. They say that despite the use of a few prayers and occasional quotations from the Koran, he relies mainly on the Bible and that his doctrines are directly opposed to Moslem doctrines and purely a personal matter."[22]

Indeed, in years past, in Philadelphia, for example, there has been physical violence between blacks following orthodox Islam and those blacks following Muhammad's brand. However, in recent years, the organization has carefully avoided notoriety and clashes with the police. Intent upon establishing their own territory or state, and securing a firmer grip upon the economy, the Muslims are presently at their highest peak, with fifty-one mosques scattered throughout twenty-four states and the District of Columbia. They broadcast on forty-seven different radio stations and have a television program in Washington, D.C. They own bakeries, dry cleaners, restaurants, farmland, livestock, jewelry shops, barber shops, and supermarkets, and have their own printing plant and parochial school system in Chicago.

Thus, in spite of their many enemies; in spite of a strained relationship with orthodox Islam; in spite of dissension and splintering caused by Malcolm X's break and assassination, the Black Muslims appear to be here to stay. Washington said, "Their growth is possible because they dramatize the deprivation of the Negro, thereby attracting disillusioned members from other cults and congregations." And said Lincoln: "They will continue to expand as long as racial tension is permitted to flourish in America."

THE WORD "BLACK" IN THE BIBLE

In the King James Version of the Old Testament, seven different Hebrew words are translated "black." One word speaks of a black marble stone (Est 1:6). A second word, whose meaning to Hebrew scholars is doubtful, probably means to glow or to illuminate with anxiety or dread (Joel 2:6). A third word is literally "pupil of the eye" (Pr 7:9). A fourth word means to be dark. It is sometimes used when referring to the darkness of the skies, the clouds, the sun, or the moon. It is most often used, however, in a figurative sense and speaks of mourning, sadness, lament, depression and despair. Eighteen verses use this word in this manner.

One interesting verse is Job 30:28: "I went mourning without the sun." This is better rendered: "I go about blackened but not by the sun." The classic verse using this particular word is Jeremiah 8:21, "For the hurt of the daughter of my people am I hurt; *I am black;* astonishment hath taken hold on me." This scripture is used as support to prove that Jeremiah was a black man. However, a complete reading of chapter 8 will reveal the metaphorical use of blackness signifying despair is in keeping with the context, and this verse should not be cited as a proof text that Jeremiah was a black man.

A fifth Hebrew word translated "black" means to grow warm and tender, to be or grow hot. Lamentations 5:10 reads: "Our skin was black like an oven because of the terrible famine." This could be rendered: "Our skin has become hot like a furnace, because of the famine." A sixth Hebrew word meaning to be or grow dark is used in Lamentations 4:8. "Their visage is blacker than a coal." Once again the context shows that the dark visage is not a racial characteristic but depicts misery and calamity. This same verse contains the seventh Hebrew word and is translated "coal." Thus the verse could be rendered: "Their visage is darker than blackness." There are two oft-cited scriptures containing this particular word. One is Job 30:30, "My skin is black upon me, and my bones are burned with heat." Once more the Hebrew idea of blackness describes calamity and sorrow. A reading of Job 29 and 30 will support this interpretation. The primary purpose of the statement, "My skin is black upon me," is to describe a strong feeling of despondency.

The second scripture containing this word is better known. It is found in Song of Solomon 1:5-6: "I am black, but comely, O ye daughters of Jerusalem, as the tents of Kedar, as the curtains of Solomon. Look not upon me, *because I am black,* because the sun hath looked upon me: my mother's children were angry with me; they made me the keeper of the vineyards; but mine own vineyard have I not kept." Note that it is not Solomon but the Shulamite woman who is described as black.

C. Herbert Oliver in his book *No Flesh Shall Glory* points out that the word "but" in the verse "I am black, but comely" should be "and"—"I am black and comely."[23] The Hebrew conjunction may mean either "but" or "and," and the context will help determine which is proper. This Bedouin woman compared herself with the women living in the city, and explained her swarthiness or darkness as the result of the sun beating down upon her while she worked in the vineyards, a task forced upon her by her lazy brothers. She lamented the fact that she failed to take care of her own complexion.

In the New Testament, attention is drawn to Revelation 1:14, "His head and his hairs were white like wool, as white as snow." With this verse some claim that Jesus Christ, according to the flesh, was a Negro. Surely, they say, John's description of Christ having woolly hair could mean only one thing—Jesus was a black man. However, the phrase "white like wool" does not refer to the material of the hair. It refers to the color. If I say, "Your shirt is green like grass," it does not mean you have on a grass shirt. The whiteness is the thing stressed in Revelation 1:14, and it symbolizes two things: (1) holiness—purity and glory, (2) age—wisdom and eternity. Jesus Christ is the Ancient of Days. Furthermore, if one insists that this scripture means Jesus' hair was woolly, what is there to prevent us from believing His hair was also cold and icy, like snow?

The attempts to prove that Job, Jeremiah, and Jesus Christ were black men are futile. And basically, it is not important, for in God's sight no flesh shall glory (1 Co 1:29). The racial-superiority myth is a false crutch, and the pride of skin color or race is unworthy of the Christian. It is too bad that some have let their attitudes on race spoil their witness of Christ, forcing those whom they feel are inferior to search the scriptures, not for salvation or edification, but for some basis upon which to establish their own brand of race supremacy. The fact remains, in spite of white and black supremacists, God is no respecter of faces or races. It is not the color of a man's skin that counts, but whether he has been cleansed by the precious blood of the Lord Jesus Christ. Any religion based upon the color of a man's skin is not biblical. And if it is not biblical, it is not of God.

6

REVOLUTION: 1954-?

CIVIL DISOBEDIENCE

THE BIBLE TEACHES OBEDIENCE TO THE GOVERNMENT

In this age of protest, "civil disobedience" is a commonly heard term. Of late, many articles have been written by government officials, jurists, and churchmen. What constitutes civil disobedience and whether it is legal, moral, biblical, constructive, or destructive are matters which divide men. Christians, too, from different denominations and within the same denominations, vary in their opinions and beliefs.

Church members most strongly committed to a social gospel are those most willing to engage in civil disobedience. This is not difficult to understand because the twin evils of worldliness and materialism cause men to emphasize the physical, the temporal, the here and now, making them less and less concerned about the spiritual and the hereafter. Indeed, "strangers and pilgrims" are titles calculated to make many modern churchgoers squirm in their pews. In love with this world, men will go to any lengths to make this world a better place in which to live. And many reckon that civil disobedience is one method by which to achieve this goal.

What basis should the Christian use for determining his views on civil disobedience? The Bible must be his standard, and it has some very definite things to say on the subject:

> Romans 13:1-5: Let every soul be subject unto the higher powers. For there is no power but of God: the powers that be are ordained of God. Whosoever therefore resisteth the power, resisteth the ordinance of God: and they that resist shall receive to themselves damnation. For rulers are not a terror to good works, but to the evil. Wilt thou then not be

74

afraid of the power? Do that which is good, and thou shalt have praise of the same: for he is the minister of God to thee for good. But if thou do that which is evil, be afraid; for he beareth not the sword in vain; for he is the minister of God, a revenger to execute wrath upon him that doeth evil. Wherefore, ye must needs be subject, not only for wrath, but also for conscience sake.

Titus 3:1: Put them in mind to be subject to principalities and powers; to obey magistrates, to be ready to every good work.

1 Peter 2:13-16: Submit yourselves to every ordinance of man for the Lord's sake: whether it be to the king, as supreme; or unto governors, as unto them that are sent by him for the punishment of evildoers, and for the praise of them that do well. For so is the will of God, that with well doing ye may put to silence the ignorance of foolish men: as free, and not using your liberty for a cloke of maliciousness, but as the servants of God.

In these passages the saint is exhorted to make a definite decision to maintain a heart attitude and adopt the policy of submission to human authority.

ARE THERE ANY EXCEPTIONS?

The question comes: Is there ever a time when the saint must disobey his government? The answer is yes. And the exception is based primarily upon several New Testament verses. First is the phrase in 1 Peter 2:13, "every ordinance of man" or every human institution or creation. This is further expanded by our Lord in Matthew 22:21, "Render therefore unto Caesar the things which are Caesar's; and unto God the things that are God's." It is absolutely imperative that the Bible believer understand what is taught here.

There are some things which God has not given to men to rule over. These things don't belong to Caesar; they are outside governmental jurisdiction. So when men seek to rule in these areas not given them by God, then the Christian has every right to disobey. "As long as government stays within its realm, the Christian is to render his obedience. . . . What they (secular governments) cannot legitimately do is tell the people of God what their doctrines must be, or how or with whom they may or may not worship and minister."[1]

PHARAOH AND THE MOTHER OF MOSES

Consider the following cases: When a pharaoh arose over Egypt who knew not Joseph, the children of Israel were treated harshly. Eventually they were made slaves. When they continued to prosper, the king first ordered the midwives to kill every male baby born of the Jews; later he ordered all his people to cast every son into the river, but to save every daughter (Ex 1:22). Jochebed, the mother of Moses, hid her baby boy for three months; then, when she could no longer hide him, she made an ark out of bulrushes, daubed it with slime and pitch, and put the child in it. She then placed the basket among the reeds at the river's brink. You know the rest of the story. Would you call the action of the midwives and Jochebed civil disobedience?

Nothing in the Bible teaches that a government has the right to take the lives of innocent babies. This was not war; this was infanticide (Mt 2:16). This was not capital punishment; this was murder. And as such it was outside of the pharaoh's province and jurisdiction to command. "But the midwives feared God, and did not as the king of Egypt commanded them, but saved the male children alive" (Ex 1:17).

KING DARIUS AND DANIEL

King Darius set 120 princes or satraps over his kingdom, and over them were placed three presidents. Daniel was one of these presidents. Soon distinguished above the others because of his excellent spirit, Daniel was preferred above them all, and the king was considering setting him over the whole realm. Envious and jealous, the others sought to find some ground for complaint against Daniel; but they could not. Then they connived to get the king to sign a decree making it unlawful for any man to make petition or prayer to any god or man for thirty days. This bit of flattery appealed to Darius and he signed the order.

"Now when Daniel knew that the writing was signed, he went into his house; and his windows being open in his chamber toward Jerusalem, he kneeled upon his knees three times a day, and prayed, and gave thanks before his God, as he did aforetime" (Dan 6:10). The conspirators found him doing so, reported him to the king, and Daniel was thrown into the den of lions. Civil disobedience? Here again the principle holds. No man, be he king, pharaoh, president, or dictator, has the authority from God to determine when and to whom another man should pray. This is not in Caesar's realm.[2]

THE PERSECUTION OF THE APOSTLES

One afternoon Peter and John saw a man who had been lame since birth sitting at the gate of the temple which is called Beautiful. By the power of the Holy Spirit, and in the name of Jesus Christ, the man was healed. This started a tumult; priests, the captain of the temple, and the Sadducees came upon the crowd that had gathered and was listening to Peter preach. Peter and John were thrown into prison. The next day, when the high priest, Annas, and Caiaphas, John, Alexander, and all the other members of the high priest's family were gathered together at Jerusalem, Peter and John were questioned. Peter spoke, and the healed man was right there.

Nonplussed, the council had a private meeting; their decision was to threaten the apostles and command them to speak henceforth to no man in this name. But Peter and John answered, "Whether it be right in the sight of God to hearken unto you more than unto God, judge ye. For we cannot but speak the things which we have seen and heard" (Ac 4:19-20). After the two disciples returned to the other Christians, they all prayed and asked for more power, more boldness to speak the Word. And with great power they witnessed of Christ's resurrection. In fact, so much was done that the high priest and his men again laid hold of the apostles and threw them in prison. However, the angel of the Lord opened the prison doors at night, and brought them forth, saying, "Go, stand and speak in the temple to the people all the words of this life" (Ac 5:20). And so they did.

By then, the high priest and the various councils and senates had gathered, and they sent to the prison for the apostles. The prison officials returned and informed them that the prison doors were shut; the guards were there, but when they opened the cell doors, nobody was there. Then someone came and reported that the Christians were standing in the temple, preaching and teaching the gospel. Brought before them again, the high priest said, "We gave you strict orders not to continue teaching in this name, and behold, you have filled Jerusalem with your teaching, and intend to bring this man's blood upon us. But Peter and the apostles answered and said 'We must obey God rather than men' " (Ac 5:28-29).

CONTEMPORARY CIVIL DISOBEDIENCE NOT SCRIPTURAL

These stories are a far cry from the activity which is called civil disobedience today. In fact, there's something disturbing about comparing today's acts of civil disobedience with these biblical incidents. Civil disobedience is defined as the deliberate, nonviolent refusal to obey a law believed immoral, unconstitutional, or unjust, and the willingness to accept penalties for that violation. However, this definition is not adequate for the Bible believer because it is humanist-oriented. Whereas the individuals in the Bible alleged to have committed civil disobedience were basically interested in the spiritual aspects of life—praying, preaching and teaching the good news of the Lord Jesus Christ, worshiping and lifting up the holy name of God—this cannot be truthfully said of contemporary civil-disobedience advocates. The emphasis today is basically materialistic.

Certainly moral issues are involved; no one denies this. But the contemporary civil-disobedience advocate who withholds taxes, legally pickets, or illegally marches, does so not because he has been proscribed or limited in his worship of God or Christ, but because *he* deems certain laws and acts of the government to be immoral or unjust.

DR. MARTIN LUTHER KING, JR.

One of the foremost exponents of civil disobedience was the late Dr. Martin Luther King, Jr.[3] When his philosophies are examined and studied in the light of the Scriptures, they are found to fall short of the will of Christ. And there is no hesitation here in criticizing Dr. King's beliefs. It is naïve to suggest that all Negroes should think alike simply because they *are* Negroes. God's Word and will are more important than so-called "black unity." In his "Letter from Birmingham City Jail," Dr. King wrote, "There are just laws and there are unjust laws. I would be the first to advocate obeying just laws. One has not only a legal but moral responsibility to obey just laws. Conversely, one has a moral responsibility to disobey unjust laws." On another occasion Dr. King said, "Civil Disobedience is something that can be justified when a man's conscience tells him it [a law] is unjust."

The danger here is subjectivism. Who determines which laws are unjust and which are just? Thoreau? Gandhi? Each individual who feels so led? But male and female may differ in opinion about the justness or inequality of any given law. So may black and white, majority and minority, educated and illiterate, driver and pedestrian, poor man and rich man, young and old, Northerner and Southerner, Protestant and Roman Catholic, management and labor. And so it goes. Reliance upon conscience is not always a solution to the problem, for conscience is *not* an infallible guide. It may be weak or defiled. The consciences of some Christians also need more enlightenment through sound Bible study and prayer. Some consciences of unbelievers are seared and cauterized. The governor of Mississippi may honestly and conscientiously believe that all Negroes constitute an inferior race; another man may in all good conscience accept drugs as a part of his religion.

Some people think that being submissive to the penalty is important in any definition of civil disobedience. But this willingness to be punished means nothing. Paul said that those who oppose authority will receive condemnation upon themselves (Ro 13:2*b*). Yes, "woe unto them who decree unrighteous decrees" (Is 10:1), and God will judge them. But woe unto them who violate these unjust laws! The Christian must remember that Satan is still the prince of this world system and that this present age is evil. In light of such world conditions and leadership, all men share and participate in an evil system; the only escape is to go out of this world altogether (1 Co 5:10). Furthermore, it cannot be claimed that the unavailability or ineffectiveness of democratic means or institutions to make right social wrongs thereby justifies civil disobedience. This too is fraught with dangers.

NAÏVETÉ AND IGNORANCE OF CIVIL-DISOBEDIENCE ADVOCATES

Social gospelers in general, and advocates of civil disobedience in particular, are naïve about human nature. They fail miserably to reckon with the deceitfulness of the human heart. For example: (1) Any contribution to the breakdown of authority on one front adds to the potential of breakdown of authority in other areas of life: home, family, school, church, etc. (2) The civil-disobedience advocate does not consider the fact that he may be influencing others who are not made of the same moral stuff. (3) Similarly, to state, as did Dr. King, that if violence occurs, it will be nonviolently accepted, does not consider the civil-disobedience advocate's partial responsibility for the violence in the first place. (4) What is considered harmless and legal—such as boycotts and mass picketing—can easily become injurious and illegitimate power plays of extortion, the iron fist hid under a velvet glove. (5) The martyr complex which states, "I'll take the consequences," will begin to wear thin. When no changes are made with respect to the unjust law, civil-disobedience advocates will find that the self-control and self-discipline required under stress is beyond the old nature's capability of giving. The result cannot help but be violence! These are some of the reasons why we firmly believe that civil disobedience logically pursued leads to chaos, confusion, and anarchy.

SUMMARY: THE PROPER APPROACH

Caesar has no authority over the human soul. No one can forbid another to worship Jesus Christ. And it must be admitted that thus far in America no one has officially prevented black Christians from worshiping Christ. Yes, there have been jim-crow buses; we have had to eat in segregated restaurants. But we said grace and ate. Yes, there are churches and schools which refuse to admit black believers. Such churches are respecters of persons, prejudiced, and more concerned with tradition and social customs than they are with obeying God's Word. And it bothers me that some of these very Christians tell in glowing terms how God is able to deliver them from the shackles of alcohol and nicotine, but evidently the same Lord is not able to deliver them from the ignorance of racial prejudice.

The truth remains: these things do not hinder and have not hindered many Christians from serving the Lord. They need not adversely affect a man's relationship to or with

Christ. If anything, the man who is surrendered to God will find that men's suppressive acts, their illegal measures, their exploitation, frauds, hypocrisies and unrighteous decrees can all be taken by God and used to draw the humble soul closer to Christ. The black Christian in America is not prevented from worshiping Jesus Christ by immoral or unjust laws of segregation, disfranchisement, jim crow, restrictive housing covenants, etc. Therefore, rather than give any encouragement to civil disobedience, Christians should be encouraged to practice the grace of giving up, that moderation of Christ which is to be made known to all men. Humility and surrender to the Holy Spirit, rather than civil disobedience, ought to be stressed.

True freedom, real freedom, is found only in submission to the Lord Jesus. It cannot be achieved through men's efforts. We must not let politics take the place of the Holy Spirit, for God is neither a Republican nor a Democrat. We must not let patriotism take the place of the Holy Spirit, for God is not an American. Democracy will increasingly prove a failure because men's hearts are evil and incurably sick. That is why Christians are warned to not make their freedom a pretext for misconduct. Our freedoms as Americans—free speech, the right to peaceful assembly, etc.—must not become a screen for evildoing. Abuse of such freedom only serves to give unbelievers a basis for criticism. Scripture says the best way to silence their criticism is by doing good things (1 Pe 2:15). That is why it is contradictory to break a law and claim to be fighting for freedom. True freedom is found only in doing God's will. In this case, it is His will that we submit to the powers that be; and such submission is the act of a free man.

BLACK POWER

A BLACK DEFINITION OF BLACK POWER

The story is told that when a Los Angeles white man showed up at the Public Assistance Bureau for Welfare Aid, he was received by a Negro receptionist, given information by a Negro clerk, interviewed by a Negro interviewer, and assigned to a Negro caseworker. The result: he got angry and kicked out the glass front door of the building. After he

was caught by a Negro gateman, arrested by a Negro police-
man, booked by a Negro sergeant, sentenced by a Negro
judge, and rushed off to jail by a Negro transportation officer,
he muttered: "It's black everywhere!"

How's that for a definition of black power? The fact is,
however, if you ask a hundred different people to tell you
what the term means you probably would hear a hundred
different definitions. The phrase had been used some years
ago by the Negro novelist, Richard Wright, but it catapulted
into prominence when it dropped from the lips of Stokely
Carmichael in June, 1966. The Baptist from Bimini, Adam
Clayton Powell, said, "Black Power depends on how you
define it. It's fragmented." Floyd McKissick stated that black
power means: (1) the growth of political power, (2) building of economic power, (3) improvement of self-image, (4)
development of leadership, (5) encouragement of federal
law enforcement, (6) mobilization of consumer power.

Stokely Carmichael said it means political power, with
Negroes "taking over the power structure according to the
democratic process" in areas where Negroes outnumber
whites. Where Negroes are outnumbered, they must organize
"independently outside both parties, then move into those
parties as a strong block vote" to force politicians to heed
Negro demands. They must build a "power base so strong
that whites will be brought to their knees whenever they
mess with us."[4] Dr. J. H. Cone defines black power as "complete emancipation of black people from white oppression by
whatever means black people deem necessary. . . black freedom, black self-determination. . . it is an attitude, an inward
affirmation of the essential worth of blackness."[5]

Thus, black power is defined as the ability to push whites
around, to reject their support, to take over everything, to be
destructive, burn, fight, and riot. Obviously such concepts
reinforce the white man's feelings of insecurity, for he sees
black power as a repudiation of nonviolence. On the other
hand, a more positive and constructive approach to black
power would say that it is the ability to bargain with whites
instead of begging from them; it is dignity, pride, self-respect,
self-determination, self-identity, racial solidarity, in-groupness,
equality, or political and cultural and economic influence.

GOALS OF BLACK POWER

Black power "promises a new identity, a new dignity, to men who can accept their blackness. . . to deliver men from helplessness and apathy if they will appropriate their history as a black people."[6] Preston Williams says, "Black Power seeks first to gain black control in order to mitigate if not abolish, the effects of white racism. Secondly, it seeks to transform the Negro value system so that blacks will not aid whites to victimize blacks. . . . The major thrust then of the Black Power movement is the reorientation of the Negro value system and re-creation of black communal life."[7] Again, Dr. Cone goes so far as to state that black power is consistent with the gospel of Jesus Christ: "Indeed, I have even suggested that if Christ is present among the oppressed, as he promised, he must be working through the activity of Black Power."[8]

CRITICISMS OF THE BLACK-POWER MOVEMENT

On the other hand, there are those people who feel that the black-power advocates are not very realistic in their goals of rejection of cooperation with the whites. Kenneth Clark called the black-power movement "a bitter retreat from the possibility of the attainment of the goals of any serious racial integration in America. . . [it] has a no-win premise, is ambiguous, an attempt to make a verbal virtue of involuntary racial segregation. It is the sour-grapes phenomenon on the American racial scene."[9]

Dr. William T. Fontaine, University of Pennsylvania black professor, concludes that the black-power movement actually promotes a greater racial separation and commits the Negro struggle for social justice into the hands of irresponsible elements. The slogan stirs up resentment in whites similar to that which blacks feel when they hear the phrase "white supremacy."

BLACK POWER'S COUNTERPART: WHITE BACKLASH

Some years ago when the term "white backlash" was in vogue, I stated that what many call a "white backlash" was in reality no more than an unveiling of the evil in the white man's heart. For many years, indeed for centuries, the Negroes in this country have suffered from exploitation, segregation, disfranchisement, rape, and lynching. The mentality that produced such criminal treatment, as well as the white power structure and the attitude of racial superiority, still remains. And all attempts to justify withholding equal rights because of "Negro rioting" are based upon faulty reasoning. One gets the impression upon hearing the term "white backlash" that the white man, good fellow that he is, was all set to display his magnanimity, benevolence and fairness until Negroes started to riot. This is a false picture. Indeed, talk of a white backlash is no more than a rationalization for doing what the heart wants to do.

In the battle against the evils of the white-power structure, we tend to forget that there is within the black man's heart that which would soon establish, given the opportunity, a black-power structure. In other words, black tyranny and black oppression would show itself. For, without Christ, black power is merely the power of black people to do evil; it is the ability of an unregenerate man whose skin happens to be black to express what is in his sinful heart. As pointed out earlier, most victims of crimes committed by blacks are blacks themselves. Of course, the black-power advocates would insist that the white man has so brainwashed us that we hate ourselves and that is why we kill off each other. But, whatever the psychology behind self-destructiveness in black people, it falls within the scope of wickedness and serves to support the Bible truth that man's heart is wicked, regardless of the color of his skin.

BLACK POWER IS AN EXPRESSION OF PRIDE

It is difficult to understand how a Christian black can be willing to espouse black power, knowing that it offends other Christians, white and black. R. W. Terry points out that nearly 40 percent of whites believe black power means black rule over whites and that white response to the slogan is overwhelmingly negative: "Most whites feel threatened, bewildered, upset and angry because of heightened militancy in the black community."[10] The slogan alienates, separates, and increases resentment. Furthermore, black power smacks of race pride. And the pride of skin color is a false crutch; it is unworthy of the Christian.

Why boast of something or be proud of something over which you have had no control? It points out the foolishness of race pride. If you had nothing to do with choosing your race, why should you feel proud or inferior because of your race? Seen in this light, it is just as ridiculous to talk about black power as it would be for all blue-eyed people to band together and shout, "Blue-eye Power!"

The cry of black power contradicts the very things which the Bible teaches: love one another, let each esteem others better than himself, seek peace and pursue it, be kind and humble with one another. Therefore, no Christian should be part of such a movement. In God's presence no flesh shall glory (1 Co 1:29).

BLACK POWER IS AN EXPRESSION OF HUMANISM

Basically, the black-power movement is another form of humanism: a mode or attitude of thought or action centering upon distinctively human interests or ideals to be accomplished by man's intellect and strength. As such, it belongs to the world, the cosmos, that order or system which, though ruled by the devil, has man as its center; and which—by its unbelief, air of independence, lack of realism, and spiritual blindness—demonstrates its evil opposition to God. The cosmos is composed of those people, pursuits, pleasures, purposes, and places where Jesus Christ is not wanted. In short, the attitude expressed by the black-power movement belongs to that which is headed by Satan, hates Christians, and is passing away.

True power is the ability to do good. Doing good in a bad world requires good men. And without Jesus Christ no man can be or do good in God's sight. Man has no such power, according to the Bible: "God hath spoken once; twice have I heard this; that power belongeth unto God" (Ps 62:11). Even those who hold to a more constructive and positive force as the true meaning of black power must understand that what they seek for black people cannot be achieved through black power but only through Jesus Christ who loved us and gave Himself for us. It is not black power, but Holy Spirit power: "Not by might, nor by power, but by my spirit, said the LORD of hosts" (Zec 4:6*b*).

BLACK THEOLOGY

THE MEANING OF BLACK THEOLOGY

Geddes Hanson has defined black theology as "a process. . . a self-conscious effort to relate the experience of
American blackness to the corpus [main body] of Christian
theology. . . [which] represents a determination to re-form
the assumption of mainstream Protestant theology by relating
seriously the peculiarities of the black experience in America
to the gospel of a living Messiah who shares the broadest
dimension of that experience."[11]

It is tied in with black power, for, says Dr. Cone, "Black
power, the power of the black man to say yes to his own
'black being,' and to make the other accept him or be prepared for a struggle, is the fullest sign that Jesus is alive."
Recently in Detroit the Black Christian Nationalist Movement
met at the Shrine of the Black Madonna. The Reverend Albert B. Cleage, Jr., host pastor and founder of the movement,
said that Negro congregations have to "develop a theology
grounded in black history."

From the viewpoint of the black Evangelical, true theology
is grounded in the Bible; it is based upon the teachings of the
Scriptures. And since the God of the Bible is the Creator of
all men, He knows what all men need, regardless of their skin
color or race or their experiences in life. Indeed, Jesus Christ
died for all men, all races. The Negro's experience in America
is no worse than that which some other peoples have ex-
perienced in history. Only pride puffs up a man and makes
him think he must have a special theology to fit his case and
condition.

Furthermore, getting free from the white man and still re-
maining a slave to self and the old sin nature is a waste of
time. Therefore, black theology, which emphasizes the destruction of white racism (in a purely negative manner, showing no love for the white man and offering nothing constructive), is a waste of time; it offers no freedom from the racism
and shackles of sin in the black man's heart.

Dr. Cone's work, *Black Theology and Black Power,* is full
of concepts which are contrary to the teachings of the Bible;
to refute his position point by point would require another
book. His use of Scripture and the name of Jesus Christ

makes all the more subtle the perversion of the gospel and all the more dangerous the idea of black theology. White racism is but one expression of sin in the human heart. Although I am a black man, born in America, hardly able to view life except through the eyes of Ghetto Joe, the Holy Spirit helps me "keep my cool" and view life more objectively than many Negroes. Black theology is not objective; it wants me to take the Bible and Jesus Christ and mash them through the fine mesh screen of the black man's experience in America. Dr. Cone denies making Christ secondary to the experience of black oppression, but his denial is not convincing.

Again, I am simply amazed at the social gospeler and the black-power and black-theology advocates' naïveté concerning man's sin nature. Somehow, those who have but faintly grasped the concept of man's depravity, have likewise weakly laid hold of the meaning of Christ's atoning work. The diligent Bible student knows that, sinwise, all men are the same. What is true of one race is true of all races with respect to their ruin in sin and their needed remedy in Christ. A theology which seeks to change outward circumstances and the attitudes of sinful men without first seeking an inner change in its adherents is, in essence, not a theology but a humanology. And not a very good one at that!

BLACK REPARATIONS

MANY BLACKS THINK FAVORABLY OF THE IDEA

There is nothing Christian about the Black Manifesto and Introduction (see Appendix A) produced by the National Black Economic Development Conference in Detroit on April 26, 1969. And of course no one claims that it is Christian. But many black ministers, even some black Evangelicals, have given their approval to the "thrust" of the documents. Indeed, some are in wholehearted agreement with the idea of reparations.

The Reverend Calvin B. Marshall, chairman of the National Black Economic Conference, said, "We are seeking what is justly the black man's. Nobody can say the black man has not been systematically deprived. The whole concept of reparations is theologically sound." The Reverend Ralph Abernathy, head of the Southern Christian Leadership Conference, said, "Now God has sent us a crude but determined prophet to plague us to repentance, and we debate his language, his methods, and ignore his message." We wonder what god the Reverend Abernathy is talking about. The late Whitney Young of the Urban League said, "It is a valid concept in balancing the scales for centuries of injustice."

SOME BLACK LEADERS REJECT IT

Fortunately, not all black leaders have been taken in by this concept. Bayard Rustin said, "Nobody owes me anything." Reparations is an attractive idea because it calls for justice. However, while it condemns, it does not correct social injustice. Furthermore, said Rustin, "Guilt is an uncomfortable emotion, and the guilty party will rationalize his sins and affirm them as virtues. By such a process, today's ally can become tomorrow's enemy."[12] Dr. J. H. Jackson, president of the National Baptist Convention, regards the manifesto as a "totalitarian message" which would "destroy religious freedom."

Those who advocate such payments are playing upon the white man's feelings of fear and guilt. This is unworthy of the Christian. But one black Evangelical told me he was not concerned about the white man's heart or motives; all that mattered was for the white man to take his foot off our people's neck now, or else! Of course, some suggest that here is an opportunity for white churches to spiritually purify themselves.

BIBLE SUPPORT FOR THE IDEA OF REPARATIONS?

Some claim that Egypt paid the Israelites reparations and that God was the prime mover in such payments; therefore, there is a basis for black reparations. Exodus 12:35-36 (ASV) reads: "And the children of Israel did according to the word of Moses; and they asked of the Egyptians jewels of silver, and jewels of gold, and raiment: and Jehovah gave the people favor in the sight of the Egyptians, so that they let them have what they asked. And they despoiled the Egyptians."

There is always danger in reaching into the Bible and pulling something out of context and then applying it to ourselves. The Israelites were the chosen people of God; American Negroes can make no such claim (though some men have been deluded into believing that blacks are the *original* Jews). Also, the Israelites were leaving Egypt; American Negroes intend to remain in America, although some whites wish otherwise and possibly, like the Egyptians, would be glad to donate funds for our relocation. In addition, all the firstborn of Egypt had been killed; there was not a house of the Egyptians where there was not one dead. The Egyptians at this point were more than glad to get rid of the Israelites and Moses!

Some claim that the story of Zacchaeus (Lk 19:1-10) supports the demand for reparations. But Zacchaeus had a change of heart, brought about by a personal encounter with the Lord Jesus. The whites from whom reparations are sought, for the most part, have had no such encounter or change of heart.

Second, Zacchaeus' act was voluntary; most whites today are resisting the demand. Third, Zacchaeus was involved *personally*. He *personally* confessed and restored fourfold to those he had *personally* defrauded. The demand for reparations is highly impersonal and amounts to guilt by association. It leaps over generations and indicts the entire white population.

Although some contributions for reparations have been given by individual churches and groups—often as the result of demonstrations interrupting worship services—not a great deal has come thus far from the Black Manifesto.

EVIL SIDE EFFECTS

The demand for reparations has detrimental side effects in that it perpetuates the very paternalistic spirit which blacks vehemently denounce, it produces even more arrogance for blacks who consider the payment of such money by whites as a sign of weakness, and it increases materialistic greed, suggesting that money is a cure-all and that, given a sufficient amount, we will solve the race problem. But money without love is a snare. The truth is, the masses of white *unbelievers* owe me nothing.

But white believers do owe me something. In fact, we owe each other something—love (Ro 13:8). Money is no substitute for this love born of the Holy Spirit and manifested in Christlike attitudes, concern, speech, and deeds. How true to the Adamic nature that men should demand that which does not belong to them, yet reject that which God so freely gives: salvation through belief in the shed blood of Jesus Christ.

Thus, civil disobedience, black power, black theology, and reparations from whites are not to be the black Christian's chief concern, despite the injustices which Negroes have suffered in America over the centuries. These things will not solve prejudice, discrimination, and the other evils of our society. Only Christ can change a man; therefore, the black believer must devote his time, energy, and money to bringing men—both black and white—to Christ.

7

THE SOCIAL GOSPEL
AND THE BLACK PREACHER

THE TASK OF THE CHURCH IN THE TWENTIETH CENTURY

The post-World War II period has brought dramatic changes in the religious life of the American Negro. Emphasis is on the social gospel, the institutional-type church, the civil rights struggle, economic boycotts, black power, black reparations, and black theology, which are some of the major thrusts of the present era.

The first thing we are bound to ask regarding the social gospel is, What is the role of the church? and How is this role determined? The church or local assembly is the place where Christians come together in order to fellowship, pray, study the Bible, worship and praise God in spirit and in truth; we are to receive instruction and exhortation to witness and present Christ everywhere—at home, school, work, or play.

It is a fact that the gospel of Jesus Christ has social implications. This cannot be denied. And that Evangelicals need to be more concerned about society as a whole is a criticism we accept. But to strike the proper balance and emphasis seems to be a difficult task. Moberg, for example, fails to see the New Testament priority when he states, "It is only as persons are born again by the Holy Spirit that they become spiritual children of God, but the gospel of Jesus Christ has far-reaching social implications. . . . Soul winning and social concern go hand in hand in the Christian faith."[1]

Social concern should never be put on the same level with soul-winning. God's kingdom and God's righteousness in Christ are still to be sought *first*. The failure to understand and obey the Word of God, our only source for determining the role of the church and its primary emphasis, is at the root of the social gospeler's dilemma. Take, for example, the institutional-type church. It is really not too far from the description of the "Negro church" given by DuBois at the turn of the century. Thus, the emphasis is not new. But, in keeping with the general trend in America, some blacks have become overly occupied, indeed, almost obsessed, with the physical, the material, the temporal, the here and now. They see as the ideal church the one that is "doing something"—the institutional type of church.

Major projects found in these kinds of local assemblies are: credit unions, consumer-information bureaus; job training and job opportunity or placement services; Boy and Girl Scout troops; bowling or basketball teams and interchurch leagues; day-care centers, nurseries, Get-Set or Head-Start programs; tutoring classes; old folks' homes; ambulance corps and blood banks; sewing factories, specializing in choir and clergy robes; low-rent housing projects, cooperative apartments and supermarkets; legal aid; prenatal and birth-control clinics; community centers open for recreation, some including even chaperoned dancing. And so it goes.

Many of these things (not all) are good—in their places. But is the church "their place"? And why is it true that in the majority of such institutional-type assemblies the gospel of Jesus Christ is not preached?

MINISTRIES OF THE PROPHETS AND JESUS CHRIST

The ideal social gospeler is the preacher who seeks to establish an institutional-type church, stresses the here and now, engages in politics, fights for civil rights, and believes in black power, black reparations, and black theology. Unfortunately, he thinks that Christ's ministry on earth is a good basis for his own emphasis and activity. He also lays claim to the acts of Old Testament prophets. However, the prophets' social teachings and Christ's physical healing ministry are not criteria for determining the church's role in society.

The only adequate corrective is a true biblical/historical understanding of God at work in history—and the role He has given the church. In order to ascertain the role of the church, its job, its calling, one must study the letters to the churches of Rome, Galatia, Philippi, etc., not the Old Testament prophets or the gospels. Refusal to accept a dispensational view of history, with its emphasis on the role of the New Testament church over against the nation/state of Israel, is one cause of the social gospeler's misplaced emphasis. The Old Testament prophets were under the law; they dealt with an apostate nation, and manifested their social concern by their convicting preaching against the wicked politicians, priests and people of their day. There was no church then, but a society which, having known the will of God through the prophets and having fallen into idolatry, consequently lost its social concern with respect to the poor, orphans, widows, and the oppressed.

Social gospelers are fond of the synoptics. Of course Christ was concerned about the poor and needy; He fed the hungry multitudes. But He also turned water into wine, calmed an angry ocean, gave sight to the blind, cast out demons, walked on water, cleansed lepers, and raised the dead.

Yet, the greater things given to the church are none of the above (Jn 14:12). Rather, the task of the church is to win individuals to the Christ who performed these miracles. The Lord's main purpose in coming was to die on the cross for our sins. The healings and social concern shown during His earthly ministry are insignificant compared with Calvary. And the social gospeler who forgets this fact plays down the atonement and the necessity of the death of Christ.

THE ROLE OF THE CHRISTIAN MINISTER

What is the minister's task? Undoubtedly the answer depends on what he accepts as his basis of authority. If he accepts the Bible as God's Word, he should have no trouble discovering his role as a Christian minister. But if he sees the Bible as the work of mere men, he will stir up a hornet's nest of varying opinions, speculation, and confusion.

The Bible is the Word of God, and this is what it says about the job of the preacher:

> Mark 16:15—Go ye into all the world, and preach the gospel to every creature.

> Acts 6:4—But we will give ourselves continually to prayer, and to the ministry of the word.

> Acts 26:18—To open their eyes, and to turn them from darkness to light, and from the power of Satan unto God, that they may receive forgiveness of sins, and inheritance among them which are sanctified by faith that is in me [Christ].

> 1 Corinthians 1:17—For Christ sent me not to baptize, but to preach the gospel: not with wisdom of words, lest the cross of Christ should be made of none effect.

> Ephesians 4:11-12—And he gave some, apostles; and some, prophets; and some, evangelists; and some, pastors and teachers; for the perfecting of the saints, for the work of the ministry, for the edifying of the body of Christ.

> 2 Timothy 4:2—Preach the word; be instant in season, out of season: reprove, rebuke, exhort with all longsuffering and doctrine.

The pastorals—1 and 2 Timothy and Titus—are invaluable here. Just these few scriptures make it obvious that the minister of God has his work defined for him by the Word of God—not by science, not by politics, not by governmental decree, tradition, public opinion, not by society in general, and not by any particular group in society, be it racial, regional, economical, professional, etc. Of course, there are those who ignore the Bible and proffer, unsolicited, their concepts of what the preacher should do. For example:

> The Negro minister who wishes to keep in time with his people is going to have to put his full weight behind the drive for full and equal political rights for his flock. . . . To get the Negro back into the Church, ministers are going to have to take a more active part across the nation in proving they are "with us." They are going to have to go to the people in the slums as well as in the middle class neighborhoods. This is the challenge to our churches.[2]

Accepting the challenge, Negro preachers have moved into the forefront of the civil rights struggle; they attempt to make their religion "relevant" by serving, they say, the "whole man."

> In the contemporary struggle for civil rights, the church is the main institution through which social dissatisfactions and civil aspirations can be expressed . . . In many communities, especially in the South, the Negro church is the only institution capable of working for civil rights at all. Because of its independent support and its relative freedom from governmental intimidation, the Negro church is often the center of protest meetings, voter registration projects and other mass efforts.[3]

Some Negro ministers have become so involved in the civil rights' struggle that perhaps they could be better called politicians, sociologists, religious humanists, or religious philosophers rather than preachers of the gospel. They seem totally unaware that "No man that warreth entangleth himself with the affairs of this life; that he may please him who hath chosen him to be a soldier" (2 Ti 2:4).

THE "WHOLE MAN" PHILOSOPHY

What about the "whole man"? God Himself has ordained a division of labor under which each man has a job to do, and each has his own calling. To ignore this fact is to be impractical and, for all their efforts at practicality, those who fail to understand human nature from the Bible perspective find that their efforts are doomed to failure from the start. I wouldn't go to my dentist to have rubber heels put on my shoes. I wouldn't go to my automobile mechanic to get a shot of penicillin. Each man has his own work, and in this sense he cannot be all things to all men.[4] No man is smart enough for that. Albert Schweitzer was a brilliant man: author, philosopher, missionary, organist and organ-builder, musicologist, medical doctor, theologian. Yet, with all his brilliance, his theology leaves much to be desired. So not even the genius is able to satisfy every aspect of man's needs.

SPIRITUAL THINGS ARE MOST IMPORTANT

The preacher has not been called by God to be a politician, lawyer, civil rights activist, antipoverty campaigner, etc. The apostles would not leave their work to serve tables. "It is not desirable for us," they said, "to neglect the word of God in order to serve tables" (Ac 6:2, NASB). The role of the Christian preacher has not changed since the days of Paul because the human heart has not changed. It is still deceitful. We are still born in sin, shaped in iniquity, and in dire need of a Saviour, who is Jesus Christ alone. Electronics, computerization, laser beams, heart transplants, supersonic flights, and lunar landings have not changed the human heart one iota. No matter what else we obtain in life, we need God, for God has so fixed it that we are not to live by bread alone.

The primary and most essential need is that of the soul and spirit. And I think the black man has to be asked all over again, What shall it profit a man, a black man, to win

the whole world and lose his own soul? Too many preachers
are leaving the work God called them to do, and they are
seeking to accomplish something He did not call them to do.
I do not question their sincerity or impugn the motives of any
who disagree with me, but when a minister begins to emphasize the temporal, the mundane, the purely physical and
racial, rather than the spiritual and the eternal, he undermines the work of Christ and the purpose of the Holy Spirit.

The social gospeler who thinks that changing the environment and raising the standards of living is the answer is badly
mistaken. It cannot be proven that better environment produces better morals. Nor are poor people the worst moral
characters. The social-gospel preacher must learn that he has
been called to deal with that part of man which is most important. He must not prostitute his calling by dabbling in politics and stressing the physical aspects of life. Failure here will
show that he does not fully understand the honor bestowed
on him by God who called him into the Christian ministry.
What most men mean when they say the "whole man" is the
physical and material part of man. Without proper spiritual
guidance the "whole man" suffers. This is the way God made
us, and it is foolish to buck it by majoring in minors. Dr.
Hugh Thompson Kerr said that we are sent not to preach
sociology but salvation; not economics but evangelism; not
reform but redemption; not culture but conversion; not progress but pardon; not the social order but the new birth;
not an organization but a new creation; not democracy, but
the Gospel; not civilization but Christ; we are ambassadors,
not diplomats.

Don't get the idea that the evangelical Christian minister
is unmindful of bad conditions; no Christian in his right
mind approves of rioting, slums, prejudice, racial bias, or
segregation; nor are we unmoved by war, poverty, crime,
hunger, and unemployment. But the preacher should know
that the root of these evils is sin. For example, one root of
poverty is laziness; another root is greed. As long as there
are lazy men and greedy men, there will be poverty. And the
preacher is called to deal with the root, not only the leaves.

All attempts to improve society will fail unless the hearts
of men are changed. Boycotts or selective patronage, sit-ins,
picketing, and mass demonstrations are all carnal weapons of

the world, calculated to achieve certain carnal, external, materialistic ends, but which have no beneficial effect upon the heart. All action by Christians which is unconcerned about a man's soul, unconcerned whether he accepts the shed blood of Christ, of necessity is an action which belongs to this world system, a system which is evil, passing away, hates Christians, and is ruled by the devil.

SOCIAL GOSPELER TREADS DANGEROUS GROUND

The minister must not let his hands be tied either by bad habits or bad associations. Clean living is more effective than racial activity. Nor should politics be allowed to tie up the preacher. He is to judge society, not let society dictate to him. He is to keep his hands clean, free, and unfettered. That way he can condemn not only the evil white man, but the evil black man as well. If the preacher will stick to his calling and preach the gospel of the Lord Jesus Christ, seek to win the lost, build up the saved, and allow himself to be used of the Lord to change hearts, he will be a good minister of Jesus Christ. Then the hearers, the members of the church, with the Word of God in their souls, can go out into society, into these various fields, to exhibit the love of Christ, to work to alleviate some of the misery, penury and ignorance in this cruel world, and to win others to a saving knowledge of the Lord. It is a very practical truth that the conscientious minister discovers he has a full-time job on his hands in sticking to his calling as outlined for him in the Scriptures.

What we have said here is not mere theory. We have seen the effects of the social-gospel emphasis; we have seen its fruits. And we don't like what we see: the dried-up spirits, the lack of joy in the pursuit of nothingness (material goods); the bitterness, the disappointment even in "success"; the need for a continuous shot in the arm to keep up flagging spirits and jaded souls! So the social-gospel church and preacher stand guilty not only of blurring the vision of Jesus Christ and losing sight of the purpose of the church, but also of producing a bunch of spiritual sadsacks. L. Nelson Bell's words are appropriate at this point:

> To her [the church] alone has been committed the message of salvation from sin. Above all else she is the repository of the gospel of the Lord Jesus Christ, and it is her duty to

preach it at home and abroad. Any emphasis for secular matters without a corresponding conviction of the content of the Gospel message is a deviation which harms the Church and detracts from her influence in the secular world which she has been commissioned by her Lord to reach.[5]

OTHER FAULTS OF THE SOCIAL GOSPELER

The black social-gospel preacher is fond of spotlighting the sins of the white power structure, and there is much talk about the sins of society and corporate guilt (this is a basis for black reparations). However, little if anything is said about the sins of the individuals who make up their congregations.

The failure to preach the Bible has helped produce a people who cannot discern right from wrong. Though they are church members, they are Bible illiterates. Unable to discern God's will for their individual personal lives, obviously these social-gospel church members cannot rightly ascertain God's will for the local assembly or corporate church. The social-gospel preacher underestimates the power of the preached Word, and considers its effects and results too slow or unimportant. It is better, however, to be slow and pleasing to the Lord than to try shortcut methods in human strength and to displease God.

What is moral about civil disobedience as defined and practiced by the modern social gospeler? What is right about Christians picketing or boycotting another man's business, and jeopardizing the jobs of others? Can we justify harming a few for what we consider the good of many? Or harming whites for the good of blacks? This may be good Robin Hood theology, but it is not New Testamental. We must not do evil that good may come out of it. To actively prevent a man from conducting his legitimate business is evil; worse, to be unconcerned about that man's relationship with Jesus Christ is wrong; so, whether by commission or omission, we do not please God. If you cannot fit Romans 12:21 (NASB) into your deeds, then it is best not to commit them: "Be not overcome by evil, but overcome evil with good."

However, what is advocated here is for Christians only. The appeal is to the saint, not to the unbeliever. The masses of blacks are either ignorant of Christ or have rejected Him.

I mention this because a common mistake made by professed Christian leaders is the failure to discern who is in the crowd.

Too many social gospelers ignore the doctrine of separation. Because they seek a common social or racial goal, they join others who seek the same or are willing to help; it does not matter who they are or what their motives are or what beliefs they hold. Agnostics, skeptics, atheists, unitarians, Muslims, Communists, non-Evangelicals—it doesn't matter, as long as they are with us on this race thing!

This lack of separation is one of the reasons many social gospelers, while having a form of godliness, deny the power of God in their personal lives. Lack of discernment and the ability to determine right and wrong is seen in the ministry of an outstanding black social-gospel preacher, the Reverend Leon H. Sullivan.[6] His blasphemous words in regard to Father Divine were quoted earlier. In March, 1970, this same minister collected $528.00 from members of the Zion Baptist Church in Philadelphia as a donation to the Black Muslims! Now, undoubtedly all black Americans resent the fact that whites in Alabama shot and poisoned Black Muslim cattle, slowing up the Muslims' commendable efforts at self-support. But the Black Muslims are the avowed enemies of Christianity. Is racial solidarity stronger than our love for the Saviour? What are we primarily: black men or Christians? How blind must be the pastor and members of any Christian church which gives money to the Black Muslims!

ESCHATOLOGY AND THE SOCIAL GOSPELER

Eschatology is the social gospeler's downfall. We have not suggested and do not recommend a do-nothing attitude concerning social problems. To accuse the black Evangelical of this is to make a false accusation. But belief in the proper eschatology (doctrine of the last things) does affect our ideas about social concern, and the way we express that concern is influenced by our eschatological viewpoints.

The Evangelical recognizes that the world system is in the lap of the devil, and that injustice, war, poverty, and prejudice are all parts of the system. But the social gospeler appears to be deluded. He thinks God has left it up to man to make the world a better place in which to live. Surely there is little evidence today that man is succeeding. Indeed, the idea of

man's improving the world is not biblical. It is a poor concept, certainly not based upon the truths of the Scriptures,
and it has led some men to assume roles God never intended
or called them to have. God's plan is to let things get worse
and worse (2 Ti 3:13), and only the return of Jesus Christ
will alter world conditions for the better. The social gospeler's
failure at this point finds him seeking an imaginary pot of
gold at the end of the rainbow of humanism.

EVIL SIDE EFFECTS OF FLIRTING WITH THE WORLD

Finally, concerning the social gospel, the church's flirtation
with the world is not without its evil side effects. Inasmuch
as Satan hates the church, he seeks only to use it in such a
way as to thwart God's plan and purpose for the church. The
world despises the Bible, and the devil seeks to undermine its
authority. But emphasizing this-worldliness, social gospelers
have fallen into Satan's trap, and it has affected their own
personal lives and the life of the church as a whole.

For example, when preachers stress educational, social or
economic matters, and job training and racial advancement,
it is always at the expense of personal devotions and prayer
life and Bible study. Some think they can combine a Christ-
centered, Bible-centered ministry with social and civic activities; but, practically speaking, it never works out. It's like trying to serve two masters. These men spread themselves so thin
that soon their spiritual ministry becomes nil. Such is the demand of the world for the preacher's attention, time, and
energy. Even counseling, visitation, and sermon preparation
are adversely affected. As for their churches, like priest like
people. They are not missions-minded, nor are they interested
in evangelism.

Such assemblies (and many have large memberships) are
not known for producing missionaries, Bible teachers, evangelists, and outstanding Christian character. Their outlook on
life becomes even more this-worldly and materialistic. In a
very subtle way, black racism is spawned, hatred for the white
man is increased. Statistics point to a waning influence in
what we have labeled the "black church." How strange that
even with such materialistic emphasis, the social gospeler
fails to attract and keep the masses of blacks who come look-
ing for a bowl of social-gospel soup.

8

THE AMERICAN NEGRO'S CONTRIBUTIONS TO THE CHURCH

MISSIONS

THE OVERALL PICTURE

Generally speaking, the picture of missions in the black church is not very bright. Joseph Washington writes:

> Negroes are fantastically difficult to recruit in any endeavor which includes sustained sacrifice for the well-being of others. . . . From the earliest days to the present, Negro missionary work has been directed only at people of color, and the quality of missions continues to be inferior to that accomplished by "mainstream" denominations. . . . Where there has been missionary fervor, it has been racially oriented, being concerned not with the mission of the Church but with the work of the denominations.[1]

Having considered already the background of black religion, the low state of missions is not too surprising. Indeed, we marvel that we have any missionaries at all. It shows that God is able and the power of the Holy Spirit is not to be underestimated.

I do not know the total number of black American missionaries now serving throughout the world. Liberia, West Africa, because of its open-door policy, has the highest proportion of black American missionaries currently on the field. Black American missionaries are also serving in Ghana, Nigeria, Congo, Sudan, Sierra Leone, and parts of East Africa. They are also found in New Guinea, Japan, Jamaica, Haiti, the Bahamas, Brazil, as well as in Central America.

They are from various denominations: African Methodist Episcopal, as well as AME Zion; National Baptist, USA, Inc.;

101

Progressive Baptist; Seventh-Day Adventist; Church of God in Christ; and various Holiness and Pentecostal groups. They are from organizations like the Afro-American Missionary Crusade, the Carver Foreign Missions Board, the Lott Carey Board, and other independent boards.

THE AFRICAN METHODIST EPISCOPAL AND AMEZ CHURCHES

In 1821 the Reverend Daniel Coker went to West Africa with the first group of people sent out by the American Colonization Society. However, there is no record of an AME church being established by Coker. Perhaps the actual beginning of direct foreign missionary work was that of the Reverend Scipio Beanes who sailed for Haiti in 1827. The AME church has stations today in West Africa, South Africa, the Caribbean, South America, and Canada.[2]

The AME Zion Church started its foreign missionary work in Liberia, West Africa, when the Reverend and Mrs. Andrew Cartwright of Elizabeth City, North Carolina, sailed from New York City in 1876. This denomination has stations in the Gold Coast, Nigeria, British Guiana (Guyana), the Virgin Islands, and other places.

THE NATIONAL BAPTIST CONVENTION FOREIGN MISSION BOARD

The largest work to be found among Negro Americans is the Foreign Mission Board of the National Baptist Convention, USA, Inc.:

> Despite the handicaps of being a slave or a freeman in a slave-oriented society, the first state-wide organization among the few churches that existed in 1836 was the Providence Missionary Baptist District Association of Ohio. The aim of this organization was to send missionaries back to Africa. Until the issuance of the Emancipation Proclamation, there were at least six national organizations among Negro Baptists whose sole objective was African Missions.

> In 1879, Reverend W. W. Colley of Virginia, who had served as a Missionary in Africa under the Foreign Mission Board of the Southern Baptist Convention, returned to the U.S. imbued with the desire of awakening Negro Baptists to a greater love for God and Africa. He spent much time canvassing the States and met hundreds of Pastors stressing this great need.

Finally, in Montgomery, Alabama—on November 24th, 1880, one hundred and fifty-one delegates representing eleven States brought the Foreign Mission Convention of the U.S.A. into being. As a result of this organization, six missionaries were immediately sent to the Republic of Liberia, Cape Mount County, near the village of Bendoo, to open the first organized Baptist Mission Station since Emancipation.

For the next fifteen years twelve missionaries served on this field. Two of them died within six months following their arrival; five others had to return with their health irreparably damaged.

In 1894, representatives of the Foreign Mission Convention met with representatives from two other national Negro bodies, namely, the American National Baptist Convention, then eight years old, and the National Educational Convention, then two years old, and resolved to consolidate into one national body, and this was effected in Atlanta, Georgia, in 1895.

The Foreign Mission Board continued the operations of the Foreign Mission Convention, and the Board of Christian Education perpetuated the work of the National Educational Convention. In this way, our National Baptist Convention of the U.S.A., Incorporated, was born.

Today, the Foreign Mission Board operates in six countries on the Continent of Africa: Sierra Leone, Liberia, Ghana, Malawi, the Republic of South Africa, and the Republic of Lesotho; in Nicaragua, Central America and the Bahama Islands. There are twelve major stations, many of which serve as the center for five hundred and nine outer stations and churches with a present membership of forty-four thousand, fifty-one members.

Seventeen hundred and thirty-three students in our elementary and high schools are now being served, and thirty-two young men are being trained in our Seminary in the Republic of Lesotho. Our medical services in Liberia and Malawi record over 19,000 treatments annually. The Board underwrites the salaries of three hundred and ninety-seven missionaries and native workers, of which nineteen are American Negroes.[3]

The total contribution for the fiscal year ending June 30, 1970, was $252,787.17. This amount of money, and nineteen black American missionaries are not much for an organization of 6.4 million membership. But as has been said earlier, we did not have much to work with. I think we must agree with Dr. Harvey:

> All we have endeavored to do is to open your minds to a few gleams of truth which for the most part have been hidden under a blanket of discriminatory silence. Despite our isolation from the main currents of American life, despite our lack of educational opportunities, despite our economic inequalities and cultural disadvantages, despite our fight to live, to survive in a racist America, the Negro Baptist was still motivated by that Great Commission which the Lord Jesus entrusted to all believers.
>
> Over the years we are aware of the many short-comings, failures and weaknesses displayed in some of our Missionary endeavors, but we do rejoice in the achievements, however humble, and the Negro National Baptist Convention, Inc., comprising six million odd members and twenty-eight thousand odd churches, shall continue this noble service for the extension of the Kingdom of God.[4]

THE LOTT CAREY MISSIONARY CONVENTION

The first American Negro missionary was George Liele (mentioned in chap. 2), who sailed to Jamaica and began a work. Lott Carey was the second. An ex-slave from Virginia, he sailed in 1821 to Liberia, where he founded the First Baptist Church of Monrovia in 1822. This church still exists today and is known as the Providence Baptist Church. When a group of leaders in the National Baptist Convention felt that more should be done for missions, they left that organization and founded the Lott Carey Convention in December, 1897. It presently has about fifteen missionaries in three fields.[5]

BLACK AMERICAN MISSIONARIES UNDER
WHITE MISSION BOARDS

Nearly all mission boards deserve condemnation for refusing in the past to accept American Negroes as missionaries. Now things are changing. The rising tide of nationalism and racism is pushing out the white man in many areas. Some mission boards are beginning to see the light. William Pannell says that white Evangelicals "function fairly well among themselves, holding their nice conferences, going to their nice churches, founding their nice camps for children. It gets funny when they announce the Annual Missions Conference. What can be more informative for a black man than to sit on a missions confab sponsored by a church that just moved away from you."[6]

In his book *For This Time,* Howard Jones points out that some, perhaps many, whites believed Africans would not accept the gospel from American blacks. What an insult to the Africans, to the American Negroes, and above all, to the Holy Spirit! Pride and ignorance combine to make people do stupid things. Jones notes other problems too:

1. There are still some whites on the mission field who are prejudiced and unable to hide their true feelings against blacks.

2. There are mission officials and boards who are race-prejudiced.

3. Some are critical of the black man's ability to do a first-class job and so exhibit their paternalistic, great-white-father-complex attitude.

4. They are afraid the use of black American missionaries will lead to an increase in the number of interracial marriages.

5. They wonder whether the white churches will continue to support mission boards which use Negro missionaries.

6. Some Negroes are suspicious of the kind overtures from the white saints.

7. There is resentment; sarcastically, the question is asked: "Why all of a sudden now?"

8. A final problem: Will Negro churches support them?[7]

A WORD FROM TWO OUTSTANDING NEGRO MISSIONARY EVANGELISTS

In the January 1969 issue of the *World Vision Magazine,* Dick Hillis has written an article entitled "The Missing Black Missionary," in which he quotes Howard Jones as saying:

> Many Negro young people today would launch out in a missionary ministry if they honestly felt that their churches would faithfully stand behind them. Instead, these young people are discouraged that many of our wealthy and prospering black churches are without a vision for missions and

fail to fulfill their financial responsibility to support missions. It is equally disheartening when they see the poorer congregations that are not able to support sufficiently their ministers and the work of the church. If we expect to see an increase of black missionaries on the foreign fields, the Negro churches in America must awake to their own financial obligations to their missionaries.[8]

Bob Harrison, Overseas Crusades' Negro missionary evangelist, states practically the same thing. Agreeing with Jones that America's Negro churches must awaken to their financial obligations to their missionaries, he feels that the small number of missionary recruits from the evangelical Negro churches is partially due to the absence of a missionary program and vision in the church. But since a good percentage of Harrison's own financial support comes from black churches, large and small, he believes that if black Christians are given the right missionary exposure and are challenged with the opportunity, they will respond generously and often sacrificially. Let us pray to this end.

MUSIC

AMERICAN FOLK MUSIC: THE SPIRITUAL

If there is any one contribution made to American religion by the Negro, it is the spiritual. Negro spirituals constitute one of the finest bodies of folk songs to be found anywhere; indeed, they are considered by some as America's *only* folk music. How far back the making of spirituals by the black man in America extends is difficult to determine. J. W. Johnson says, "Indeed, the Spirituals taken as a whole contain a record and a revelation of the deeper thoughts and experiences of the Negro in this country for a period beginning three hundred years ago and covering two and a half centuries." The introduction of Christianity and the learning of English were two necessary ingredients, and perhaps roots extend back to the early eighteenth century. The establishment of the Negro's own separate place of worship was also important in determining the beginning date of the spirituals. It was not until immediately after the Civil War that whites from the North, coming into contact with blacks of the South, collected and wrote down the spirituals. Many spirituals have been lost, irretrievably so, but hundreds are extant and give us more than enough material to study and sing.[9]

ORIGIN OF THE SPIRITUALS

Some critics believe the spirituals did not originate with the black man and claim they are the white man's music. But I would agree with J. W. Johnson that spirituals are, as much as any music (especially folk music) can be, purely and solely the creation of the American Negro. Native African musical talent and rhythms combined with the knowledge of the King James Version of the Bible to produce the spiritual— not the white man's music or derivations of his hymns, and not purely African music, but something creatively new, something "forged of sorrow in the heat of religious fervor."

A viewpoint held by some is that the spirituals "ain't so spiritual." That is, they believe these songs were invented by the blacks to mislead the whites. "To the uninformed listener the words spoke of religious longing; the singing provided a harmonious accompaniment to their work, and to the viewer all was piety and submission. The true meaning of the spirituals, however, involves a communication from one to another regarding plans for escape, hostile feelings toward the master, and a general expression of rebellious attitudes."[10]

For example, these people claim that (1) "everybody talkin' 'bout heab'n ain't goin' dere" was an expression of contempt for the white man and his hypocrisy; and (2) that many of the spirituals were signals for runaway slaves. "De Gospel Train Am A-Comin" was supposedly a signal that the underground railway would operate that night. "Steal Away To Jesus" was a signal that the coast was clear for escape. "Sinner, Please Don' Let Dis Harves' Pass" was an announcement of the opportunity to escape to the North. "Let Us Praise God Together" meant that a secret meeting was to be held that midnight.[11] And so it goes.

It seems incredible that anyone could believe the spirituals were created thus. That some of the spirituals may have been used for such purposes is another matter, but to suggest they were made up for this reason is quite ridiculous. "Spirituals represent spontaneous creations of the soul in its search for comfort and escape from physical and mental turmoil."[12] James Weldon Johnson comments:

In the Spirituals the Negro did express his religious hopes and fears, his faith and his doubts. In them he also expressed his theological and ethical views, and sounded his exhortations and warnings. Songs of this character constitute the bulk of the Spirituals. But in a large proportion of the songs the Negro passed over the strict limits of religion and covered nearly the whole range of group experiences—the notable omission being sex. In many of the Spirituals the Negro gave wide play to his imagination; in them he told his stories and drew his morals therefrom; he dreamed his dreams and declared his visions; he uttered his despair and prophesied his victories; he also spoke the group wisdom and expressed the group philosophy of life.[13]

CHARACTERISTICS OF THE SPIRITUALS

The student of the Negro spirituals soon discovers some interesting facts. For instance,

1. The rhythm is often complicated, and sometimes strikingly original.

Another noticeable feature of the songs is the entire absence of triple time, or three-part measure among them. The reason for this is doubtless to be found in the beating of the foot and the swaying of the body which are such frequent accompaniments of the singing. These motions are in even measure, and in perfect time; and so it will be found that however broken and seemingly irregular the movement of the music, it is always capable of the most exact measurement. In other words, its irregularities invariably conform to the "higher law" of the perfect rhythmic law.[14]

2. They are remarkably free from any word of hatred, bitterness, anger, revenge, rebellion, or war.[15]

3. Rarely is anything humorous intended, but perhaps Negro humor is seen in some areas. On the whole, the tone of the spirituals is one of deep earnestness.

4. Negro dialect is not uniform. One man criticized me for not singing "chillun" (or "chillen") for "children" in "De Gospel Train Am A-Comin'." The fact is, dialects differed; pronunciations were not fixed. Sometimes it was not necessary to go very far in just one section of a Southern rural area to discover this. Therefore, variations are found in the spelling of the titles as well as in the texts of the spirituals.

5. There is a tremendous amount of interchanging of lines

or verses from one spiritual to another, so much so that often what is sung in the chorus has no historical, topical, or textual (biblical) relationship with the title or the first line of the spiritual.

6. Spirituals are highly subjective; most are sung in the first person. Critics of this feature of the Negro spiritual should read again the psalms of the Old Testament, especially Psalms 23, 26, and 27, and many others using the words, "I, me, my, mine."

7. They are primarily otherworldly. Mays said, "They lead one to repudiate this world, consider it a temporary abode, and look to Heaven for a complete realization of the needs and desires that are denied expression here."[16]

8. The major themes are:

a). Death. Thurman suggests that because the slave's life was held cheaply by the slave master, death was a persistent fact. Indeed, "if a slave were killed, it was merely a property loss, a matter of bookkeeping." The slave knew, of course, that death was the gateway to heaven, a place for which he longed.

b). Life. Full of loneliness, despair and suffering, life is seen as a pilgrimage, a sojourn—"I ain't got long to stay here."

c). God. Seen as a personal, intimate, and active Being, God will make all things right.

d). Judgment.

e). Heaven. The slave saw heaven as a place of joy, reunion, no slavery, and no segregation. "When I get to Heab'n, I'm going to sing and shout; there'll be nobody there to put me out!" Concerning this emphasis, Frazier said: "This philosophy represented an attitude of resignation in face of a hard fate—the struggle to make a living and realize himself in a world dominated by the white man. It was other worldly in that it looked to another world for the attainment of these ends and an escape from the evils of the present world."[17]

These emphases or characteristics are sometimes labeled as escapism, retreat from reality, or brainwashing, a soporific aimed at keeping the slave docile and submissive. The "compensatory" character of the spirituals is condemned because, although the songs helped the slave to endure his misery, they did not "necessarily motivate him to strive to eliminate the source of the ills he suffers." One wonders, however, what the slaves could have done!

GOSPEL MUSIC: DEFINITIONS AND ORIGINS

Time magazine defined the gospel song as "a spiritual with a bounce" or "sanctity with a beat." Gospel music is a mixture of spirituals and Protestant hymns and other religious songs brought North by Negroes several generations ago. Mahalia Jackson points out that in the 1920s and early 1930s, gospel music outside the South was not very well known. Large Negro churches considered it bad taste to sing religious songs with such verve because they felt it was too much like bringing nightclub jazz into the church. However, Miss Jackson and others sang in small Baptist, Pentecostal, or Holiness churches all over the country.

In his article "Soul's in. . . But Gospel's Out of Sight," Charles Hobson says,

> The current rage over "soul" disturbs some Gospel de-
> votees who feel that its mass appeal invites invidious com-
> parison with the real music of black people. But the first
> effort to water down pure Gospel for mass appeal occurred
> in the 1930's and '40's when Negro song writers like Tommy
> Dorsey, Lucie Campbell, Kenneth Morris and Roberta Mar-
> tin came up with some new material that incorporated the
> blues and jazz with standard Gospel lyrics and melodic lines.

> Meanwhile, extraordinary solo performers like Sister Ro-
> setta Thorpe, Ernestine Washington and Georgia Peach
> emerged as favorites of white listeners. By 1940, the newer
> Gospel songs and stylings had been accepted on a national
> scale. Shortly after World War II, black people started to
> purchase Gospel records in impressive numbers for the first
> time since the Depression.[18]

GOSPEL MUSIC IS BIG BUSINESS TODAY

The commercialization of gospel music is perhaps epito-
mized in and by the career of James Cleveland, singer, pianist, composer, arranger, choir director, and recording artist—"King of the Gospel."[19] He has written some 275 gospel pieces; his record album, *"Peace Be Still,"* sold over 750,-
000 copies when it was first issued. Cleveland reportedly can demand $2,000 for an appearance, is booked solid a year in

advance, and earns more than $100,000 a year. His extravagance—seen in his gold-edged stemware, fifty suits, one hundred pairs of shoes, Persian lamb overcoat, etc.—does not set well with some, and they question his sincerity and the genuineness of the gospel he sings.

Perhaps this is but one of the things which has led Joseph Washington to say that gospel music is the "most degenerate form of Negro religion." Washington claims it is the creation of a disengaged people, and has turned the freedom theme in the spiritual into licentiousness. Its rhythm detracts and distracts from the text which is practically unintelligible anyway. Gospel music is sheer entertainment practiced by commercial opportunists. Furthermore, states Washington, "Ministers who urge their people to seek their amusement in Gospel music and the hordes of singers who profit from it, lead the masses down the road of religious frenzy and escapism."[20]

GOSPELS AND NIGHTCLUBS

It is a fact that jazz bands have picked up the gospel beat and that nightclub performers have taken some of the music intact, pasted on pop words, and then boasted of the "soul" their religious background has given to their performances. It is, of course, no secret that people like Aretha Franklin, Lou Rawls, Dionne Warwick, Gladys Knight and the Pips, and the late Sam Cooke were all gospel singers at one time. Certain gospel-singing groups perform almost exclusively in nightclubs. One gospel singer said, "If rock and roll groups can 'mash-potatoes' for the Devil, then I can certainly 'twist' for Jesus." Mary Grandison of the Grandison Singers said, "People in the night clubs accept the music more than people in the churches. It's more quiet here. It's almost reverent."[21]

The jazzing up of gospel songs has not gone unnoticed or unopposed.[22] Negro pastor Dr. C.S. Stamps of the Metropolitan Baptist Church in Harlem led a group in picketing the Sweet Chariot Supper Club in the Times Square theater district in the summer of 1963. For two and a half hours they stood outside and sang spirituals in protest of the club's "prostituting of religious songs and symbols of the church."[23]

Some gospel singers also have opposed the switch to rock and roll. Dorothy Love of the famous Gospel Harmonettes said:

Many Gospel oriented singers are now enjoying tremendous success, and they use all the moans and groans you hear in Gospel. They just change the lyrics a little bit and the world goes mad. When you talk about making money, God is the last station you call. So the day I accept their offers, they'll be buying more than just my voice and talent. They'll be buying my faith . . . and there's just not enough money in the world to do that.[24]

O HAPPY DAY: MELODY OR MESSAGE?

In 1968 a twenty-five-year-old Negro composer, arranger, pianist, and conductor took the hymn, "O Happy Day," jazzed it up, and sold some 12 million copies, having made the hit parade in *Billboard*. Said Edwin Hawkins, the musician responsible for this bit of pop plagiarism, "It is good for gospel to go pop; it might bring the kids back to God."[25] The Evangelical must admit that the words of the refrain do contain a scriptural gospel message:

> O happy day, O happy day,
> When Jesus washed, Oh when he washed,
> When Jesus washed, He washed the sins away.

These are the words repeated over and over. Concerning "O Happy Day," pastor King Butler wrote:

> The quick acceptance by the pop world, and the intermingling of this record along with jazz and blues numbers should stir the thinking of Christians to ask the question: "Is it the Melody or the Message?". . . Are you aroused to new thoughts why and how a number with such a spiritual and soul-searching message could be so highly rated in the secular world without some claims of professions being made publicly of the spiritual changes that attend the lives of those persons who enjoy this song?
>
> I cannot but think of the Scriptural injunction given by the apostle Paul: ". . . I shall sing with the spirit and I shall sing with the mind also" (1 Corinthians 14:15b). Paul's point of emphasis is that there must be understanding as well as spiritual motivation (inspired by God's Spirit). Often we hear the claim that Christians should be more spiritually motivated. This is true. However, the Scriptural proof and safeguard is that there must be understanding in order for the act of praying and singing to be fruitful. Professed Christians

should be earnestly concerned about this matter of singing songs because they are popular, and then failing to understand the true message of the song.[26]

SACRED JAZZ: RATIONALIZATIONS FOR JAZZ IN THE CHURCH

In recent years jazz has made terrific headway in the black church. Some preachers, always eager to try something new, especially if it is financially profitable, have welcomed this invasion.[27] Naturally the jazz musicians justify their actions. The jazz pianist-composer, Mary Lou Williams, said, "The ability to play good jazz is a gift from God. This music is based on the spirituals—it's our only original American art form—and should be played everywhere, including church. Those who say it shouldn't be played in church do not understand they are blocking the manifestation of God's will."[28]

The famous Duke Ellington justifies his "sacred jazz" concerts this way: "Every man prays in his own language, and there is no language that God does not understand." On another occasion he said, "When a man prays, he prays in his own language. I've been playing with saxophones, trumpets, and a rhythm section for 40 years. This is my language. It's my way of praying."

"Ellington's faith may be sincere," Don Hustad remarked, "but it is obvious that his doctrinal understanding is muddled."[29] Sacred means holy, dedicated, set apart in honor of or hallowed by association with the divine. Perhaps there is the mistaken idea that because the church building has been set apart for God that whatever takes place in the church building is also sacred. However, the true character of a thing isn't changed merely by bringing it inside a church building.

MAN MUST BE TAUGHT BY GOD HOW TO WORSHIP GOD

It is simply presumptuous to think that it has been left up to men to worship God as we please. We are not to worship Him as we please, but in the way which pleases Him. The God of the Bible is to be worshiped in spirit and in truth, and not just by anybody—regardless of how good a musician is or how sincere he might be—but by men who believe that Jesus Christ died on the cross of Calvary and shed His blood for their sins.

Unfortunately there are men, preachers included, who fail to recognize this. They are blind. And our church members are blind. They no longer seem intent upon reaching the lost with the gospel of Christ, nor are they interested in edifying believers. Instead of preaching and teaching the Word of God, we have stepped aside to permit the golden hour of opportunity to be tarnished by the singing of unsanctified lips and the plink-plunk of unregenerated fingers.

THE PERVERSION OF GOD-GIVEN ABILITY

Man's ability to express himself in music is a gift from God. We do not deny this. But, like all God-given talents, music is subject to abuse and perversion. For example, language is a gift from God; misused, it becomes gossip, slander, false witnessing, and cursing. Artistic ability is God-given, but it too may degenerate into pornography. Sex is a gift from God; misused, it becomes adultery, fornication, and homosexuality.

The same is true of music. It has not escaped the blighting effect of man's immorality. God endows men with tone or pitch perception, a sense of timing or rhythm, manual dexterity, and pleasing quality of voice. But what men do with these gifts is then left up to them. Some musicians have taken these talents and misused them. The author believes jazz is one misuse; jazz is music "gone wrong."[30] The misuse of any gift is an indication both of ignorance and ingratitude—two factors which lead men into idolatry. Without question, some have made jazz their god and serve him well.

THE EFFECT OF JAZZ UPON ITS DEVOTEES

In some strange psychological manner the pronounced beat of jazz touches a responsive chord in the lower nature of men. It seems to hypnotize some of its devotees, throwing them into an uncontrollable frenzy. Their feet begin to pat, arms flail, bodies twist, and fingers snap; often these jerks and gestures are erotic and suggestive. Recent loose-jointed monkeylike dances to this music appear increasingly neurotic. The jazz beat has a definite emotional appeal, and the resulting physical reactions suggest immorality.

The exaggerated self-pity of the blues, the double entendres, and the suggestive words carelessly tread upon human emotions. Some contend that there is therapeutic value in the release of such emotional energy. However, in the long run, misdirected energy has a detrimental effect. Only when our

energies are superintended by God's Holy Spirit and chan-
neled into activities which honor Jesus Christ is there any
lasting value for all concerned.

THE FRUIT OF JAZZ: PHONINESS AND AN EARLY GRAVE

The church of Jesus Christ is the pillar and ground of the
truth; therefore it should not endorse that which is not true.
The glamour and glitter of the jazz world are as phony as a
three-dollar bill. The gaiety and laughter of the nightclub
world are hollow.

Much of jazz is show and sham. Many of the musicians are
sick and miserable inside, and some rely on dope and alcohol
to keep up the show. They sing about romance when they
mean lust; they sing about angels and heaven and paradise,
but without Christ they are on their way to hell. They sing
about love but know nothing about true love because God is
love and they are without God in Christ.

Say what you will, a tree is judged by the fruit it produces.
And the jazz tree has wormy, rotten fruit: legal scrapes, di-
vorces, alcoholism, dope and nicotine addiction, squandering
of money, paternity suits, twisted values, suicide, idolatry—
these are some of the fruits. Billie Holliday, ruined by liquor,
dope, and high living, died at the age of forty-four in a city
hospital in New York with seventy cents in her bank account.
Lester Young was dead at fifty; Albert Ammons died at forty-
two; Art Tatum was dead at forty-six; Fats Waller was dead
at thirty-nine; Bessie Smith, the great blues singer, died at
forty-two; Charlie Parker was dead at thirty-five; Dinah
Washington was about forty when she died; Sam Cooke was
dead at thirty-two; Frankie Lyman died at twenty-six; and
Jimi Hendrix was dead at twenty-six. Coleman Hawkins died
at sixty-four of pneumonia, aggravated by alcohol. Of course
there are exceptions: Duke Ellington, the late Louis Armstrong,
and some others have lived longer. But this is purely by the
grace of God. The fact remains: the majority of jazz musicians have died at an earlier age than the average person.

IS THERE A THEOLOGY OF JAZZ?

Shall we learn about God from the jazz musician? Or is
this but one more foolish attempt of man to serve God in
man's own way? Is it like Cain who sought to worship God

the way *he* wanted to worship God? The "sacred jazz" concert is of the devil and has no business in the Christian church. Hear the critics saying, "Well, jazz might as well enter the church; you've moved your gospel music into our nightclubs." True. But two wrongs don't make one right. It is not more jazz that we need, but the joy of the Holy Spirit. Not the Duke, but the King of kings, Jesus Christ. Not syncopation, but sanctification. Not improvisation, but regeneration.

JAZZ HAS NO PLACE IN THE CHURCH

The evil influence of jazz; its rotten fruit, its appeal to the Adamic nature, and the presumptuousness and idolatrous nature and Christlessness of it all lead me to say: Let it stay on the stage and in the air-conditioned nightclubs, but don't bring it into the church of Jesus Christ! The black Christian must resist the incursion of jazz into our churches, whether it be the "sacred jazz" of the Duke or the jumping gospel of a choir or chorus. Such music is not edifying for several reasons.

First of all, observance of these performers and their church audiences convinces me that they are not interested in *what* is said, but in the *way* it is said or sung. Music is supposed to be a vehicle for the words we are singing. Religious music is of value only if there is a message, and only if that message is biblical. The music is not an end in itself.[31] Words to some gospel selections are simply not good theology. It does not matter how skilled the musician, how sincere, how well trained—if the words are not true to the Scriptures, then the whole thing is a miserable, flatted flop.[32]

Second, much of what is heard in black churches is not calculated to edify, but to entertain. Edification means to make better, to build up the hearer. All that goes on in the church should be for the edification of the church members (1 Co 14:26, 40). If a believer isn't drawn closer to the Lord Jesus Christ and made more like Him through the music, then it should not be in the church. "Entertainment has never been the function of music in worship," says Dr. Lee G. Olson.

Third, those who have watched these performers cannot deny that they exalt themselves, not God, through their virtuosity, showmanship, theatricalism, and competitiveness.

Their desire to express in order to impress is backed up by their love of money, not by any desire to please Jesus Christ.

HYMNS

Lest some think these are the only musical contributions, let me hasten to bring to your attention the music of professor T. A. Dorsey, who wrote "Peace in the Valley," "Precious Lord, Take My Hand" and "When I've Done My Best." Perhaps some white Christians are unaware that the Reverend C.A. Tindley also was a Negro, a wonderful Methodist preacher, and man of God. He wrote "A Better House," "Go Wash in the Beautiful Stream," "I'll Overcome Some Day," "Leave It There," "Nothing Between," "Some Day," "Stand By Me," "The Storm Is Passing Over," "We'll Understand It Better By and By," and "What Are They Doing In Heaven?"

In summary, the religious life of America would be much the poorer were it not for the contributions in music made by the black American.

MISCELLANEOUS

With all of the faults and failures of the black American, and in spite of the author's criticisms, let us not lose sight of the positive contributions made by the Negro to America's religious life. At this point we are mindful of what the apostle Paul wrote in 2 Corinthians 4:7, "But we have this treasure in earthen vessels, that the surpassing greatness of the power may be of God and not from ourselves."

What then are some of the other contributions made by the black American to America's religious life?

1. We have seen that God raised up Negro missionaries who have gone across the face of the globe to spread the good news of Jesus Christ.

2. We noted too the musical contributions, especially the spirituals and hymns.

3. The race has produced outstanding preachers and pastors from the very beginning; they are too numerous to mention here.[33] Some of today's outstanding black evangelists are Ralph Bell, Sam Dalton, Bob Harrison, Ben Johnson, Howard O. Jones, William Pannell, Tom Skinner, Charles Williams, and Ernest Wilson. Some excellent evangelists now

pastoring are Joseph Brown, King A. Butler, B. Sam Hart, and Richard Hinton.

4. The "Negro church" has served as an outlet for the expression of emotion. It has given race leadership, strengthened family life, and, as a social center, has provided fellowship, shelter, and mutual aid. Without such an outlet under the circumstances which prevailed in slavery, much more blood would have been shed and the spiritual progress of America as a whole hindered all the more. The presence of the pagan black man gave opportunity to the various churches and denominations to manifest Christ.

Whereas many blame Christianity for numerous evils in regard to the slaves, the fact remains that some whites recognized their obligations as Christians and took advantage of the opportunity to witness for Christ. Had it not been for the genuine Christian white, the plight of the blacks would have been much worse.

5. Though I disagree with the motives, methods, and theology of many who are involved in the struggle for civil rights, it must be admitted that the social gospeler has thrust through to the heart and conscience of America to some degree. Some whites, even Evangelicals, have been made more aware of the social injustices suffered by blacks and have begun to show the concern which is proper for the Christian. Wherever poor race attitudes have been changed and improved, may Jesus Christ be praised!

6. Patience, perseverance, meekness, lack of bitterness, a high regard for the Bible, a warmth, vitality, spontaneity, lack of formality—these, I think, are some of the good qualities still found among many Negro Christians and they add to the general welfare of America's religious life. Arnold Toynbee said,

> The Negro has not, indeed, brought any ancestral religion of his own from Africa to captivate the hearts of his White fellow-citizens in America. His primitive social heritage was of so frail a texture that, save for a few shreds, it was scattered to the winds on the impact of our Western Civilization. Thus he came to America spiritually as well as physically naked; and he has met the emergency by covering his nakedness with his enslaver's cast off clothes.

The Negro has adapted himself to his new social environment by re-discovering in Christianity certain original meanings and values which Western Christendom has long ignored. Opening a simple and impressionable mind to the Gospels, he has discovered that Jesus was a prophet who came into the world not to confirm the mighty in their seats but to exalt the humble and meek. The Syrian slave immigrants who once brought Christianity into Roman Italy performed the miracle of establishing a new religion which was alive in the place of an old religion which was already dead.

It is possible that the Negro slave immigrants who have found Christianity in America may perform the greater miracle of raising the dead to life. With their childlike spiritual intuition and their genius for giving spontaneous aesthetic expression to emotional religious experience, they may perhaps be capable of kindling the cold grey ashes of Christianity which have been transmitted to them by us until, in their hearts, the divine fire glows again.

It is thus perhaps, if at all, that Christianity may conceivably become the living faith of a dying civilization for the second time. If this miracle were indeed to be performed by an American Negro Church, that would be the most dynamic response to the challenge of social penalization that has yet been made by man.[34]

7. Finally, it should be kept in mind that throughout the centuries in which the black man has been in this country, there have been those persons, however illiterate, however imperfect in their grasp of doctrine, who heard, believed, accepted the gospel and were saved. In short, the black American washed in the blood of God's dear Lamb is added to that innumerable host which will one day be manifested to the universe.

9

TRENDS AND PREDICTIONS

TRENDS

Two recent major trends apparent among black Christians are those of joining the Roman Catholic Church and of integration between white and black believers.

ROMAN CATHOLICISM

In colonial America, Roman Catholics were a minority. America was basically a Protestant country, and European immigrants seeking religious freedom desired to keep it Protestant. The Roman Catholic church has gained many converts in the United States, and in recent years its greatest gains have been made among the black populace. Prior to the twentieth century there were no concerted efforts to win the Negro to this particular denomination.[1] And that which was done met only with meager success.

There were, to be sure, limited numbers working with blacks all along, especially in Maryland and Louisiana. At best, only 5 percent of the total black population in 1865 was Roman Catholic. "The decrease in the number of Negro Catholics during the post-Civil War days was brought about by Negro independents, movements of Negroes North, lack of priests, lack of discipline of the Roman Catholic Church, and the zeal of Protestant missionaries."[2]

The total black population at the time of the Civil War was approximately 4 million, so there were about 200,000 Negro Roman Catholics at that time. By 1916 there were only 124,324, with less than a half dozen ordained Negro priests in the country. Thus there was a decline after Reconstruction in the number of black Roman Catholics. Right up

120

to the post-World War II period, the Negro had a low priority in the Roman Catholic church. In 1940 there were approximately 297,000 Negro Roman Catholics, 63.7 percent of whom were members of black churches and not of mixed or integrated churches.

By 1956 there were some 500,000 Negro Roman Catholics, an indication of the tremendous strides made among the blacks. The Catholic rate of growth is significantly greater than the growth in Protestantism, even after allowances are made for inflated statistics. Much of the overall increase in Roman Catholicism is due to the influx of Negroes, new converts to the church. Presently there are about 800,000 black Catholics, with more black priests and nuns than ever before.

Reasons for the increase. No single answer adequately explains the trend. Reasons given are:

1. The Roman Catholic church has increased its efforts to make black converts. It is a very strong church numerically in the large cities and, since the Negro continues to be drawn to urban centers (though at a slower rate recently), the growth potential of the Roman church is great.

2. As a social institution it has been quite effective. Much has been done in the way of providing food, shelter, and clothing to needy blacks.

3. There is a political aspect to the membership increase. Blacks have found employment opportunities and job advancement through their connection with the Roman Catholic church. Roman Catholic politicians have been helpful here.

4. While white Protestants in racially changing neighborhoods usually move out and build new churches in the suburbs, the Roman church remains. Furthermore, Roman Catholics have been more vocal than Protestants, especially conservative Protestants, in their official condemnation of racial discrimination as a moral sin. However, it is one thing to make a pronouncement and something else to practice what is pronounced or to enforce it. At any rate, the ear of the Negro has been caught.

Other factors are to be considered in this increase of blacks within the Roman Catholic church. Blacks themselves point out that (1) socially, some blacks consider membership in this denomination a step upward; (2) some say that Roman

Catholic services are less emotional—Generally this comment comes from more highly educated blacks who associate or equate emotionalism with ignorance; (3) accusations of low moral levels are often hurled at Negro Protestant leaders: court actions, suits, and countersuits by local churches and national conventions, splits, immorality, drunkenness, etc.; (4) the convenience of the system, with a choice of hours to attend and short services, and the liberal attitudes toward bingo and gambling, card-playing, drinking, and dancing, allow greater "freedom" to its adherents; (5) black parents claim that their children get a better education in the parochial school than in the public school.

Two other points which hold little value are (1) the authoritarian voice of Rome appeals to some blacks, and (2) whites often suggest that the church's pomp, ritual, and ceremony attract the black man.

Latest statistics: convert rate drop. The convert rate in recent days has dropped precipitously in some areas. Some say it is the result of "an image of disunity in the Church," referring to current debate over issues like the celibate priesthood and birth control. Also there is a general decline in personal faith in America in all denominations and races. Perhaps there is a possibility that the increase rate has been slowed by the black power movement.

The new influx of blacks has hit the church in the pocketbook. Complaints are voiced that the Negro is a parasite and has nothing to offer but increased statistics; Negro members are dead weight. The fact that within the last twenty years Negro membership has practically tripled is not without its problems. John T. Gillespie wrote:

> Negro pupils deepen deficits of Parish schools. Thirty years ago, only two Roman Catholic parishes in the city were mostly Negro. Today, 19 have Negro populations 60% or higher. 13 parochial schools have Negro populations in excess of 90%. 9 of them have black enrollments above 97%. This is one reason the city's Catholic schools are facing a financial crisis. The net income these parishes receive from regular weekly offerings amounts to no more than a few hundred dollars a week, hardly enough to maintain church, rectory and school, let alone pay the salaries of lay teachers and the cost of educational equipment.[3]

The following article appeared in February, 1969:

Robbing the Ghetto: How little the black people can expect from the parochial school people is being demonstrated in the proposed closing of the Catholic school and parish of St. Monica's in the Borough of Queens on Long Island. It is true that the 136-year-old property is to be taken for a public university. What is interesting is the immediate acceptance of the condemnation by the church along with an announcement that the school would be closed. The parishioners are 90% Negro. The facts are, as we have pointed out before, that the Roman Catholic Church is phasing itself out of the ghetto where school operations "do not pay." Subsidy to this church for its educational program would sharply exacerbate the imbalance in school aid. It would deprive the ghetto and reward the suburb.[4]

The black man's loss. Alignment with the Roman Catholic church with its hierarchical setup is an automatic surrender of the freedom of religious expression which blacks have enjoyed so long. Self-government is undeniably the heritage of the black church; in Roman Catholicism this is lost. Also lost is the emphasis upon preaching; a grand musical heritage is likewise forfeited. But more important is the theological situation.

This church has added poison to the truth of God's Word: works; transubstantiation; celibate priesthood; Mary's immaculate conception, perpetual virginity, assumption, and queenship of heaven; indulgences; penance; apostolic succession; the Apocrypha; baptismal regeneration; limbo and purgatory; and papal infallibility *(excathedra)*.

For many people the additive flavor goes undetected. Some do not care. Most Negroes don't know that much about doctrine one way or the other. But it is extremely important that a man believe the right things about God and Christ. And we thank God for those black Christians who, by Bible study and the guidance of the Holy Spirit, stand firm on the Rock, Christ Jesus (not Peter). They recognize the errors and false doctrine of the Roman Catholic church. Unfortunately, however, multitudes of our people have not seen the light. And Rome marches on.

INTEGRATION IN THE CHURCHES

It is doubtful that either the all-black or the all-white church will soon completely disappear. There are several reasons for this. First, there are staunch white segregationists who believe it is God's will that separate assemblies be maintained. In October 1970 in Birmingham, Alabama, a church with nearly five hundred members split over whether to admit a black woman and her eleven-year-old daughter to membership. Those favoring the effort to integrate voted to resign and form a new congregation; this was the result of months of controversy. Unfortunately, many Evangelicals are in this segregation camp. While standing for the once-for-all delivered faith, often they are guilty of the worst race relations and attitudes. Some have gone so far as to refuse admission to black American Christians in their Bible schools, camps, and universities.

Perhaps foremost is the fear of interracial marriage.[5] They talk about "racial integrity," forgetting that today some 80 percent of all American Negroes have so-called "white blood" in their veins. Very little of this came about through the union of black men with white women. The white man's concern for "racial integrity" becomes ridiculous when it is seen that whatever "racial integrity" the black man had has disappeared mainly through the efforts of white men.

Some even speak of "mongrelization." How can an evangelical Christian use such a term with respect to human beings made in the image of God and for whom Christ died? Did not the Lord make from one all nations of men? (Ac 17:26). And what is worse is the attempt to make the Bible support their beliefs. The scriptures often cited have nothing to do with racial separation but with religious separation. The unequal yoke (2 Co 6:14) is not black with white, but believer with unbeliever; yet seemingly, most white Christian parents would rather have their daughter marry a white unbeliever than a black believer. As far as interracial marriages are concerned, Hebrews 13:4 still holds true: Marriage is honorable in *all*.

Tied in with his hatred of interracial marriage is the feeling of superiority. I am in total agreement with C. H. Oliver that the basic element in opposition to interracial marriage is the feeling of race superiority.

Though many deny that they believe their race to be superior in the eyes of God, their opposition to "interracial marriage" makes their claim suspect. For behind opposition to racial intermarriage is the concept of racial solidarity. And behind the concept of racial solidarity is the concept of race preservation. Since men seek to preserve what they consider superior rather than what they deem inferior, race preservation is based upon the notion of race superiority.[6]

Second, there are those whose viewpoint is more moderate. They believe any enforced segregation is immoral, yet they caution against any enforced integration. "Take it easy," they say. "If you push too fast for church integration you will only sow the seeds of bitterness." They also say: "Well, Negroes like to live with their own kind and worship with their own people." To this, William Pannell says, "We've never had the opportunity to choose."

The result is business as usual; the status quo is maintained. Even though 90 percent of all Negro church members are Protestant, it is safe to say that, in general, white Protestants are doing little to break down segregation and to further integrate the black man in the mainstream of American society and religious life.

Third, Kenneth Clark points out that most interracial congregants are somewhat above the American mean in educational, social, and economic status. However, the blacks in the ghetto have a need which the Negro churches serve: the need for self-esteem and escape. Because there are those conditions in our society which create this need in the breast of black folks, it is doubtful if any genuinely interracial church can exist in the heart of the ghetto. Clark concludes that the church is likely to be the last of the social institutions to be effectively integrated.[7]

Fourth, that there are Negroes who resist all efforts at church integration goes without saying. They consider the church as their last and only sanctuary, the only thing they have that is their own and not the white man's. Preston Williams goes so far as to say that

the Black Church has been under continual and ceaseless attack by the White Church. From the late 40's until now the White Church has been blaming the Black Church for its

isolation and alleged inferiority. It has through its strategy
of integration attempted the destruction of the very institution
that has stood as the symbol of Black Independence. No
Black man holds a pivotal position of power in any White
religious institution, yet Whites expect every Black man in
every Black institution to surrender his real power for a
meaningless title and a few extra dollars.[8]

Some Negro ministers feel that integration is a threat to
them financially and otherwise, and so are expected to resist
any attempt to integrate their churches.

It is obvious then why it is believed total integration will
not be achieved in the near future. Whether racial segregation in the churches is officially enforced or quietly accepted
by the "silent majority," the apparent self-centeredness, self-
satisfaction, and failure to witness of the Christ who is no
respecter of persons, bring shame upon His cause.

Admittedly, there is no cause for separation when people
believe the same doctrine and profess to have the same Lord.
Time may soon come in America when persecution will drive
black and white Evangelicals to a closer fellowship. But why
wait? Why not let the world see now that Christians are indeed "soul brothers," having been cleansed by the same blood
of the same Saviour, indwelt by the same Holy Spirit, and
having the same heavenly Father!

PREDICTIONS

1. *Influence*. Generally speaking, the influence of the
church is waning. As with the whites, fewer blacks are going
into the Christian ministry. All across the country, in urban
and rural areas, Negro churches, large and small, are without
pastors. According to recent polls, churchgoing in America
has hit an all-time low. And church membership is not keeping up proportionately with the population increase.

If what is happening in Philadelphia is any criterion, the
number of major Protestant inner-city churches is shrinking.
And those left are costing more and more to maintain. It was
found that integration was not the answer, and this goal was
dropped by both black and white. The Methodists lost thirty-
five churches in Philadelphia from 1959 to 1969; the United
Presbyterians have lost eight churches in the past twenty
years; in addition, four have relocated, four merged with

suburban churches, and thirteen merged with other city churches.

Since 1960, the Episcopalians have closed seventeen city churches. The Lutherans have lost thirteen churches in the past twenty-five years. And so it goes.

2. *Respect.* Related to this is the fact that the Negro minister no longer commands the respect he once had. Allegations of immorality, too much authority, being behind the times, and failure to change with the times, are some of the indictments heard. Black ministers must not assume that there are no members in the local assembly with talent and leadership ability who could do as good a job, if not better than the minister himself, in secular pursuits.

On the other hand, more doors have opened for the Negro minister: institutional chaplaincies (hospitals, prisons, etc.); Bible schools; denominational work. These and other opportunities now give the Negro clergyman a greater variety of work and are, in small measure perhaps, responsible for the shortage of pastors.

3. *Social gospel.* No letup on the social-gospel emphasis is to be expected. The materialistic, secularist bug has bitten the black man as well as the white man in our country. Blacks are slowly forsaking their church relationships, belittling the faith of their forefathers, and increasingly becoming religious illiterates.[9] There is in the black church, as well as in America in general, a decline in religion. Economic prosperity, materialism, secularism, television, crime in the streets, the love of pleasure and recreation, the destruction of storefront churches by urban renewal and redevelopment; the competition of fraternities, secret societies, and labor unions—these are but some of the things affecting the black church and reducing its influence and power.

4. *Widening gap.* There is a slowly widening gap between black Evangelicals and black liberals or modernists: "The younger Negro minister is more highly educated secularly, though often less educated biblically, and has a greater social consciousness, but a lesser theological consciousness. His feeling is that the Negro form of fundamentalism has done mighty little for his people in the past 100 years, so he'd better emphasize something else that works."[10]

5. *Attacks on church.* Preston Williams points out that

the black church in this present period is under attack by blacks who want to show their strength, and by blacks who feel that the church is no longer relevant, no longer providing the Negro with "a meaningful explanation" of his existence. Even the black psychiatrists have thrown in their two cents:

> Religion is designed to evoke guilt, and in that regard it begins with the assumption that mortals are inherently wicked and can gain pardon and find a welcome into the house of God only by some extraordinary act of faith. An initial assumption of guilt, if taken seriously, may or may not cripple white Americans, but it is lethal to black men. . . . As discussed here, Christianity is the greatest offender, but any religion which elevates guilt-stimulating attitudes about sin and debasement to the level of the supernatural would echo this nation's attitude toward Negroes for any black man who in that religion sought comfort.[11]

6. *Mergers.* The Negro Methodists (AME, AMEZ, CME) have already taken steps to consolidate; merger is envisioned by 1972. Whether the independent-minded Baptist conventions will follow suit remains to be seen, but it is possible. The planned mergers will probably have the effect of postponing any full-fledged integration with the white churches. Those blacks in positions of authority and prestige in such merged groups may hesitate to integrate with the whites if it means loss of black authority. Then too there may be a problem, great or small, of whites accepting black leadership.

7. *Apostasy.* For the Evangelical there is but one answer: apostasy. However much liberals, social gospelers, racial activists, and others dislike the term *apostasy* or disagree with it, the Bible teaches that the visible church will end in apostasy. This should not be difficult to envision. A black man even now has to prayerfully seek a local assembly which is without gospel jazz, fashion shows, money-raising gimmicks, and condoned immorality, and, positively speaking, a church which stresses clean living, preaching of the Word, and the saving blood of Jesus Christ! To find such an assembly is no easy task.

CONCLUSION

Let not the black churchman think that his struggle against social injustice will save him. It will not. Indeed, the essential fact is that without the blood of Christ applied to their hearts, multitudes of black church members will not go up when Christ comes down. Rather, they will become a part of that vast church system (Christendom) which will be left here after the true believers are snatched up to meet Jesus Christ in the air. We close then with the words of one of our spirituals and change the one pronoun to ask you, "Where will *you* be when de "fus' trumpet soun'?"

Appendix A
The Black Manifesto

I. THE BLACK MANIFESTO INTRODUCTION

We have come from all over the country, burning with anger and despair not only with the miserable economic plight of our people, but fully aware that the racism on which the Western World was built dominates our lives. There can be no separation of the problems of racism from the problems of our economic, political, and cultural degradation. To any black man, this is clear.

But there are still some of our people who are clinging to the rhetoric of the Negro and we must separate ourselves from those Negroes who go around the country promoting all types of schemes for Black Capitalism.

Ironically, some of the most militant Black Nationalists, as they call themselves, have been the first to jump on the bandwagon of black capitalism. They are pimps, Black Power Pimps and fraudulent leaders and the people must be educated to understand that any black man or Negro who is advocating a perpetuation of capitalism inside the United States is in fact seeking not only his ultimate destruction and death, but is contributing to the exploitation of black people all around the world. For it is the power of the United States Government, this racist, imperialist government that is choking the life of all people around the world.

We are an African people. We sit back and watch the Jews in this country make Israel a powerful conservative state in the Middle East, but we are not concerned actively about the plight of our brothers in Africa. We are the most advanced technological group of black people in the world, and there are many skills that could be offered to Africa. At the same time, it must be publicly stated that many African leaders are in disarray themselves, having been duped into following the lines as laid out by the Western Imperialist governments.

Africans themselves succumbed to and are victims of the power of the United States. For instance, during the summer of 1967, as the representatives of SNCC, Howard Moore and I traveled ex-

130

tensively in Tanzania and Zambia. We talked to high, very high, government officials. We told them there were many black people in the United States who were willing to come and work in Africa. All these government officials, who were part of the leadership in their respective governments, said they wanted us to send as many skilled people that we could contact. But this program never came into fruition and we do not know the exact reasons, for I assure you that we talked and were committed to making this a successful program. It is our guess that the United States put the squeeze on these countries, for such a program directed by SNCC would have been too dangerous to the international prestige of the U.S. It is also possible that some of the wild statements by some black leader frightened the Africans.

In Africa today, there is a great suspicion of black people in this country. This is a correct suspicion since most of the Negroes who have left the States for work in Africa usually work for the Central Intelligence Agency (CIA) or the State Department. But the respect for us as a people continues to mount and the day will come when we can return to our homeland as brothers and sisters. But we should not think of going back to Africa today, for we are located in a Strategic position. We live inside the U.S. which is the *most barbaric country in the world* and we have a chance to *help bring this government down.*

Time is short and we do not have much time and it is time we stop mincing words. Caution is fine, but no oppressed people ever gained their Liberation until they were ready to fight, to use whatever means necessary, including the use of force and power of the gun to bring down the colonizer.

We have heard the rhetoric, but we have not heard the rhetoric which says that black people in this country must understand that we are the Vanguard Force. We shall liberate all the people in the U.S. and we will be instrumental in the liberation of colored people the world around. We must understand this point very clearly so that we are not trapped into diversionary and reactionary movements. Any class analysis of the U.S. shows very clearly that black people are the most oppressed group of people inside the United States. We have suffered the most from racism and exploitation, cultural degradation and lack of political power. It follows from the laws of revolution that the most oppressed will make the revolution, but we are not talking about just making the revolution. All the parties on the left who consider themselves revolutionary will say that blacks are the Vanguard, but we must assume leadership, total control and we must exercise the humanity which is inherent in us. We are the most humane people within the U.S. We have suffered and we understand suffering. Our hearts go out to the Vietnamese for we know what it is to suffer under the domination of racist America. Our hearts, our soul and all the compassion we can mount goes out to our brothers in Africa, Santa Domingo, Latin America and Asia who are being tricked by the power structure of the U.S. which is dominating the world today. These ruthless, barbaric men have systematically tried to kill all people and organizations opposed to its imperialism. We no longer can just get by with the use of the word capitalism to describe the U.S., for it is an imperial power, sending money, *missionaries* and the army throughout the world to protect this government and the few rich whites who control it. General Motors and all the major auto industries are operating in South Africa, yet the white-dominated leadership of the United Auto Workers sees no relationship to the exploitation of black people in South Africa and the exploitation of black people in the U.S. If they understand it, they certainly do not put it into practice which is the actual test. We as black people must be concerned with the total conditions of all black people in the world.

But while we talk of revolution which will be an armed confrontation and long years of sustained guerrilla warfare inside this country, we must also talk of the type of world we want to live in. We must commit ourselves to a society where the total means of production are taken from the rich and placed into the hands of the state for the welfare of all the people. This is what we mean when we say total control. And we mean that black people who have suffered the most from exploitation and racism must move to protect their black interests by assuming leadership inside of the United States of everything that exists. The time has passed when we are second in command and the white boy stands on top. This is especially true of the Welfare Agencies in this country, but it is not enough to say that a black man is on top. He must be committed to building the new society, to taking the wealth away from the rich people such as General Motors, Ford, Chrysler, the Du-Ponts, the Rockefellers, the Mellons, and all the other rich white exploiters and racists who run this world.

Where do we begin? We have already started. We started the moment we were brought to this country. In fact, we started on the shores of Africa, for we have always resisted attempts to make us slaves and now we must resist the attempts to make us capitalists. It is the financial interest of the U.S. to make us capitalists, for this will be the same line as that of integration into the mainstream of American life. Therefore, brothers and sisters, there is no need to fall into the trap that we have to get an ideology. We HAVE an ideology. Our fight is against racism, capitalism and imperialism and we are dedicated to building a socialist society inside the United States where the total means of production and distribution are in the hands of the State and that must be led by black people, by revolutionary blacks who are concerned about the total humanity of this world. And, therefore, we obviously are different from some of those who seek a black nation in the United States, for there is no way for that nation to be viable if in fact the United States remains in the hands of white racists. Then too, let us deal with some arguments that we should share power with whites. We say that there must be a revolutionary black Vanguard and that white people in this country must be willing to accept black leadership, for that is the only protection that black people have to protect ourselves from racism rising again in this country.

Racism in the U.S. is so pervasive in the mentality of whites that only an armed, well-disciplined, black-controlled government can insure the stamping out of racism in this country. And that is why we plead with black people not to be talking about a few crumbs, a few thousand dollars for this cooperative, or a thousand dollars which splits black people into fighting over the dollar. That is the intention of the government. We say . . . think in terms of total control of the U.S. Prepare ourselves to *seize state power*. Do not hedge, for time is short and all around the world the forces of liberation are directing their attacks against the U.S. It is a powerful country, but that power is not greater than that of black people. We work the chief industries in this country and we could cripple the economy while the brothers fought guerrilla warfare in the streets. This will take some long range planning, but whether it happens in a thousand years is of no consequence. It cannot happen unless we start. How then is all of this related to this conference?

First of all, this conference is called by a set of religious people, Christians, who have been involved in the exploitation and rape of black people since the country was founded. The missionary goes hand in hand with the power of the states. We must begin seizing power wherever we are and we must say to the planners of this conference that you are no longer in charge. We the people who have assembled here thank you for getting us here, but we are going to assume power over the conference and determine from this moment on the direction in which we want it to go. We are not saying that the conference was planned badly. The staff of the conference has worked hard and have done a magnificent job in bringing all of us together and we must include them in the new membership which must surface from this point on. The conference is now the property of the people who are assembled here. This we proclaim as fact and not rhetoric and there are demands that we are going to make and we insist that they help implement.

We maintain we have the revolutionary right to do this. We have the same rights, if you will, as the *Christians* had in going into Africa and raping our Motherland and bringing us away from our continent of peace and into this hostile and alien environment where we have been living in perpetual warfare since 1619.

Our seizure of power at this conference is based on a program and our program is contained in the MANIFESTO.

II. BLACK MANIFESTO

We the black people assembled in Detroit, Michigan for the National Black Economic Development Conference are fully aware that we have been forced to come together because *racist white America has exploited* our resources, our minds, our bodies, our labor. For centuries we have been forced to live as colonized people inside the United States, victimized by the most vicious, racist system in the world. We have helped to build the most industrial country in the world.

We are *therefore* demanding of the white Christian *churches* and Jewish synagogues which are part and parcel of the system of capitalism, that they begin to pay reparations to black people in this country. We are demanding $500,000,000 from the Christian white churches and the Jewish synagogues. This total comes to *15 dollars per nigger*. This is a low estimate for we maintain there are probably more than 30,000,000 black people in this country. $15 a nigger is not a large sum of money and we know that the churches and synagogues have a tremendous wealth and its membership, white America, has profited and still exploits black people. We are also not unaware that the exploitation of colored peoples around the world is aided and abetted by the white Christian churches and synagogues. This demand for $500,-000,000 is not an idle resolution or empty words. Fifteen dollars for every black brother and sister in the United States is only *a beginning* of the reparations due us as people who have been exploited and degraded, brutalized, killed and persecuted. Underneath all of this exploitation, the racism of this country had produced a psychological effect upon us that we are beginning to shake off. We are no longer afraid to demand our full rights as a people in this decadent society.

We are demanding $500,000,000 to be spent in the following way:

1. We call for the establishment of a Southern land bank to help our brothers and sisters who have to leave their land because of racist pressure for people who want to establish cooperative farms, but have no funds. We have seen too many farmers evicted from their homes because they have dared to defy the white racism of this country. We need money for land. We must fight for massive sums of money for this Southern Land Bank. We call for $200,000,000 to implement this program.

2. We call for the establishment of four major publishing and printing industries in the United States to be funded with ten million dollars each. These publishing houses are to be located in Detroit, Atlanta, Los Angeles, and New York. They will help to generate capital for further cooperative investments in the black community, provide jobs and an alternative to the white-dominated and controlled printing field.

3. We call for the establishment of four of the most advanced scientific and futuristic audio-visual networks to be located in Detroit, Chicago, Cleveland and Washington, D.C. These TV networks will provide an alternative to the racist propaganda that fills the current television networks. Each of these TV networks will be funded by ten million dollars each.

4. We call for a research skills center which will provide research on the problems of black people. This center must be funded with no less than 30 million dollars.

5. We call for the establishment of a training center for the teaching of skills in community organization, photography, movie making, television making and repair, radio building and repair and all other skills needed in communication. This training center shall be funded with no less than ten million dollars.

6. We recognize the role of the National Welfare Rights Organization and we intend to work with them. We call for ten million dollars to assist in the organization of welfare recipients. We want to organize the welfare workers in this country so that they may demand more money from the government and better administration of the welfare system of this country.

7. We call for $20,000,000 to establish a National Black Labor Strike and Defense Fund. This is necessary for the protection of black workers and their families who are fighting racist working conditions in this country.

*8. We call for the establishment of the International Black Appeal (IBA). This International Black Appeal will be funded with no less than $20,000,000. The IBA is charged with producing more capital for the establishment of co-operative businesses in the United States and Africa, our Motherland. The Interna-

tional Black Appeal is one of the most important demands that
we are making for we know that it can generate and raise funds
throughout the United States and help our African brothers. The
IBA is charged with three functions and shall be headed by James
Forman:

    (a) Raising money for the program of the National Black
        Economic Development Conference.

    (b) The development of cooperatives in African countries
        and support of African Liberation movements.

    (c) Establishment of a Black Anti-Defamation League which
        will protect our African image.

9. We call for the establishment of a Black University to be
funded with $130,000,000 to be located in the South. Negotiations
are presently under way with a Southern University.

10. We demand that IFCO allocate all unused funds in the
planning budget to implement the demands of this conference.

In order to win our demands we are aware that we will have
to have massive support, therefore:

(1) We call upon all black people throughout the United States
to consider themselves as members of the National Black Economic
Development Conference and to act in unity to help force the
racist white Christian churches and Jewish synagogues to implement these demands.

(2) We call upon all the concerned black people across the
country to contact black workers, black women, black students and
the black unemployed, community groups, welfare organizations,
teacher organizations, church leaders and organizations explaining
how these demands are vital to the black community of the U. S.
Pressure by whatever means necessary should be applied to the
white power structure of the racist white Christian churches and
Jewish synagogues. All black people should act boldly in confront-
ing our white oppressors and demanding this modest reparation
of 15 dollars per black man.

(3) Delegates and members of the National Black Economic
Development Conference are urged to call press conferences in
the cities and to attempt to get as many black organizations as
possible to support the demands of the conference. The quick use
of the press in the local areas will heighten the tension and these
demands must be attempted to be won in a short period of time,
although we are prepared for protracted and long range struggle.

(4) We call for the total disruption of selected church sponsored agencies operating anywhere in the U.S. and the world. Black
workers, black women, black students and the black unemployed
*Revised and approved by Steering Committee.

are encouraged to seize the offices, telephones, and printing apparatus of all church sponsored agencies and to hold these in trusteeship until our demands are met.

(5) We call upon all delegates and members of the National Black Economic Development Conference to stage sit-in demonstrations at selected black and white churches. This is not to be interpreted as a continuation of the sit-in movement of the early sixties but we know that active confrontation inside white churches is possible and will strengthen the possibility of meeting our demands. Such confrontation can take the form of reading the Black Manifesto instead of a sermon or passing it out to church members. The principle of self-defense should be applied if attacked.

(6) On May 4, 1969, or a date thereafter, depending upon local conditions, we call upon black people to commence the disruption of the racist churches and synagogues throughout the United States.

(7) We call upon IFCO to serve as a central staff to coordinate the mandate of the conference and to reproduce and distribute en mass literature, leaflets, news items, press releases and other material.

(8) We call upon all delegates to find within the white community those forces which will work under the leadership of blacks to implement these demands by whatever means necessary. By taking such actions, white Americans will demonstrate concretely that they are willing to fight the white skin privilege and the white supremacy and racism which has forced us as black people to make these demands.

(9) We call upon all white Christians and Jews to practice patience, tolerance, understanding and nonviolence as they have encouraged, advised and demanded that we as black people should do throughout our entire enforced slavery in the United States. The true test of their faith and belief in the Cross and the words of the prophets will certainly be put to a test as we seek legitimate and extremely modest reparations for our role in developing the industrial base of the Western World through our slave labor. But we are no longer slaves, we are men and women, proud of our African heritage, determined to have our dignity.

(10) We are so proud of our African heritage and realize concretely that our struggle is not only to make revolution in the United States, but to protect our brothers and sisters in Africa and to help them rid themselves of racism, capitalism, and imperialism by whatever means necessary, including armed struggle. We are and must be willing to fight the defamation of our African

image wherever it rears its ugly head. We are therefore charging
the Steering Committee to create a Black Anti-Defamation League
to be funded by money raised from the International Black Appeal.

(11) We fully recognize that revolution in the United States
and Africa, our Motherland, is more than a one dimensional oper-
ation. It will require the total integration of the political, economic,
and military components and therefore, we call upon all our brothers and sisters who have acquired training and expertise in the
fields of engineering, electronics, research, community organization,
physics, biology, chemistry, mathematics, medicine, military science and warfare to assist the National Black Economic Development Conference in the implementation of its program.

(12) To implement these demands we must have a fearless
leadership. We must have a leadership which is willing to battle
the church establishment to implement these demands. To win our
demands we will have to declare war on the white Christian
churches and synagogues and this means we may have to fight the
total government structure of this country. Let no one here think
that these demands will be met by our mere stating them. For the
sake of the churches and synagogues, we hope that they have the
wisdom to understand that these demands are modest and reason-
able. But if the white Christians and Jews are not willing to meet
our demands through peace and good will, then we declare war
and are prepared to fight by whatever means necessary. We are,
therefore, proposing the election of the following Steering Committee:

Lucious Walker	Mark Comfort
Renny Freeman	Earl Allen
Luke Tripp	Robert Browne
Howard Fuller	Vincent Harding
James Forman	Mike Hamlin
John Watson	Len Holt
Dan Aldridge	Peter Bernard
John Williams	Michael Wright
Ken Cockrel	Muhammed Kenyatta
Chuck Wooten	Mel Jackson
Fannie Lou Hamer	Howard Moore
Julian Bond	Harold Holmes

Brothers and sisters, we no longer are shuffling our feet and
scratching our heads. We are tall, black and proud.

And we say to the white Christian churches and Jewish synagogues, to the government of this country and to all the white
racist imperialists who compose it, there is only one thing left that

you can do to further degrade black people and that is to kill us. But we have been dying too long for this country. We have died in every war. We are dying in Vietnam today fighting the wrong enemy.

The new black man wants to live and to live means that we must not become static or merely believe in self-defense. We must boldly go out and attack the white Western world at its power centers. The white Christian churches are another form of government in this country and they are used by the government of this country to exploit the people of Latin America, Asia and Africa, but the day is soon coming to an end. Therefore, brothers and sisters, the demands we make upon the white Christian churches and the Jewish synagogues are small demands. They represent 15 dollars per black person in these United States. We can legitimately demand this from the church power structure. We must demand more from the United States Government.

But to win our demands from the church which is linked up with the United States Government, we must not forget that it will ultimately be by force and power that we will win.

We are not threatening the churches. We are saying that we know the churches came with the military might of the colonizers and have been sustained by the military might of the colonizers. Hence, if the churches in colonial territories were established by military might, we know deep within our hearts that we must be prepared to use force to get our demands. We are not saying that this is the road we want to take. It is not, but let us be very clear that we are not opposed to force and we are not opposed to violence. We were captured in Africa by violence. We were kept in bondage and political servitude and forced to work as slaves by the military machinery and the Christian church working hand in hand.

We recognize that in issuing this manifesto we must prepare for a long range educational campaign in all communities of this country, but we know that the Christian churches have contributed to our oppression in white America. We do not intend to abuse our black brothers and sisters in black churches who have uncritically accepted Christianity. We want them to understand how the racist white Christian church with its hypocritical declarations and doctrines of brotherhood has abused our trust and faith. An attack on the religious beliefs of black people is not our major objective, even though we know that we were not Christians when we were brought to this country, but that Christianity was used to help enslave us. Our objective in issuing this Manifesto is to force the racist white Christian church to begin the payment of reparations which are due to all black people, not only by the Church but also by private business and the U.S. government. We see this focus on the Christian church as an effort around which all black people can unite.

Our demands are negotiable, but they cannot be minimized, they can only be increased and the Church is asked to come up with larger sums of money than we are asking. Our slogans are:

ALL ROADS MUST LEAD TO REVOLUTION
UNITE WITH WHOMEVER YOU CAN UNITE
NEUTRALIZE WHEREVER POSSIBLE
FIGHT OUR ENEMIES RELENTLESSLY
VICTORY TO THE PEOPLE
LIFE AND GOOD HEALTH TO MANKIND
RESISTANCE TO DOMINATION BY THE WHITE CHRIS-
    TIAN CHURCHES AND THE JEWISH SYNAGOGUES
REVOLUTIONARY BLACK POWER
WE SHALL WIN WITHOUT A DOUBT

Appendix B

An Outline of More Than Two Hundred Spirituals

Note the scripture references which may have been a basis for the song.

I. The Christian Life

    A. Admonition
       Don't Get Weary
       Gimme Yo' Han'
       Hear de Lambs A-Cryin' (Oh, Shepherd, feed-a my sheep): John 21:15-17
       Heav'n Boun' Soldier (Hold out yo' light): Matthew 5:14-16
       I Heard de Preachin' of de Word O' God
       If You Love God, Serve Him
       Lis'en to de Lam's
       My Ship Is on de Ocean (Po' sinner, fare you well)
       Oh, 'de Downward Road Is Crowded: Matthew 7:13
       Rise, Mourner, Rise (an' tell what de Lord has done for you)
       Run to Jesus
       Seek and Ye Shall Find: Matthew 7:7
       Singin' wid a Sword in Ma Han': Nehemiah 4:13-18
       Stay in de Field ('til de war is ended)
       Steal away to Jesus
       Too Late (sinnah, carry de key an' gone home; Massa Jesus lock de do')
       Walk Together, Children: Amos 3:3
       Walk You in de Light: 1 John 1:7
       You Go, I'll Go wid You (Open yo' mouth, I'll speak for you): Exodus 3:12; 4:12
       You Mus' Hab dat True Religion (you can't cross dere, de ribbuh ob Jordan)

B. Aspirations
    De Winter'll Soon Be Over
    Don't Leave Me, Lord (Don't leave-a me behin')
    Down by the River
    Fighting On (we are almost down to de shore)
    Gimme dat Ol'-Time Religion
    Give Me Jesus
    Good Lord, Shall I Ever Be de One? (to get over in
       de Promise' Lan'?)
    Good News, de Chariot's Comin' (I don't want her to
       leave-a me behind): 2 Kings 2:11
    Gwineter Ride up in de Chariot Soon-a in de Mornin':
       2 Kings 2:11
    I Ain't Gwineter Study War (no mo'): Isaiah 2:4
    I Am Goin' to Join in this Army
    I'm Gwine to Jine de Great 'Sociation
    Let de Heaven Light Shine on Me
    Look away (in de heaven, Lord)
    Lord, I Want to be a Christian in-a My Heart
    Religion Is a Fortune I Really Do Believe
    Sun Don't Set in de Mornin' (Light shine round de
       worl')
    We Am Clim'in' Jacob's Ladder: Genesis 28:12
    We Are Walking in de Light: 1 John 1:7 (If religion
       was a thing dat money could buy, de rich would live
       and de po' would die)
    Who'll Be a Witness for My Lord?

C. Life's Pilgrimage (on the way to heaven)
    De Ol Sheep Done Know de Road (De young lam's
       mus' fin' de way)
    Don't Be Weary, Traveler (come along home to Jesus)
    Gwineter Sing All Along de Way
    I Don't Wan' to Stay Here No Longer
    I'm A-Rollin'
    I'm Just A-Going over Jordan (Pilgrim's Song)
    Keep A-Inchin' Along
    Leanin' on de Lord (How'd ye feel when ye come out
       de wilderness)
    Lord, Until I Reach My Home (I never 'spect to give
       the journey over)
    Mos' Done Trabelling
    Oh, Jerusalem (Oh, my Lord! I'm walkin' de road)
    Oh, My Good Lord, Show Me de Way: John 14:5

Oh, Stand the Storm (It won't be long, we'll anchor by and by)

Poor Pilgrim (I heard of a city called heaven, I'm strivin' to make it my home)

Roll de Ol' Chariot Along (ef ye don't hang on behin')

Until I Reach-a Ma Home (I nevah inten' to give de journey ovah)

We Are Almost Home

Weary Traveler (Let us cheer the . . .)

D.   Salvation (Repentance, Conversion)
Bright Sparkles in de Churchyard
Chilly Water (Hallelujah to dat Lam')
De Angels in Heab'n Gwineter Write My Name: Luke 10:20
Done Foun' My Los' Sheep: Luke 15:3-7
I Got a Home in-a dat Rock: Exodus 17:5; 1 Corinthians 10:4
I Know de Lord's Laid His Hands on Me
My Soul's Been Anchored in de Lord
Po' Mourner's Got a Home at Las'

E.   Present Deliverance and Past Judgment
Didn't My Lord Deliver Daniel: Daniel 6:23
Didn't Ol' Pharaoh Get Los' (in de Red Sea): Exodus 14:27
Go Down, Moses: Exodus 5:1
God's A-Gwineter Trouble de Water (Wade in de Water): Exodus 14
He's Jus' de Same Today: Hebrews 13:8
Hol' de Win' Don't Let It Blow
I Thank God I'm Free at Last
Joshua Fit de Battle ob Jericho: Joshua 6
My Lord Delibered Daniel: Daniel 6
Oh, Freedom
Ride on, Moses
Slav'r Chain (don broke at las')

F.   Prayer
A Little Talk wid Jesus Makes It Right
Dere's a Little Wheel A-Turnin' in My Heart
Ev'ry Time I Feel de Spirit
I Couldn't Hear Nobody Pray
I've Been A-List'ning All de Night Long (to hear some sinner pray)

It's Me, O Lord (standin' in the need o' prayer)
Oh, Hear Me Prayin' (I want to be more holy ev'ry day)
Prayer Is de Key of Heab'n (Faith unlocks de do')
When I Fall on My Knees

G.   Tribulation
Hard Trials: John 16:33
I'm So Glad Trouble Don't Last Alway
I'm Troubled in Mind
Keep Me F'om Sinkin' Down: Matthew 14:30
Members, Don't Git Weary
Mos' Done Toilin' Here
My Way's Cloudy
Nobody Knows de Trouble I See
Sometimes I Feel Like a Motherless Child
Soon I Will Be Done (a-with the troubles of the world)
Tell Jesus (done, done all I can)

H.   Miscellaneous
1. Humility
Can't You Live Humble? (to de dyin' Lam'?)
Humble Yo'self de Bell Done Ring
Gwine to Live Humble to de Lord: Matthew 18:4; 23:12
2. Praise
Hallelujah
Hear de Angels Singin'
Jubalee: Leviticus 25:10
Peter, Go Ring Dem Bells
Rise an' Shine: Isaiah 60:1
3. Obedience
I Done Done What Ya' Tol' Me to Do
4. Consolation
There Is a Balm in Gilead: Jeremiah 8:22
Up on de Mountain (I heard God talkin' Lord!)

II. Death and the Future

A.   Death
Death Come to My House, He Didn't Stay Long
Death's Gwineter Lay His Cold Icy Hands on Me
Deep River
Die in de Fiel' (I'm on my journey home)
I Feel Like My Time Ain't Long

I Want to Die Easy When I Die
In the Kingdom
Oh, de Hebben Is Shinin'
Oh, Give Way, Jordan: Joshua 3-4
Oh, Wasn't dat a Wide River?
Same Train
Swing Low, Sweet Chariot: 2 Kings 2:11
You May Bury Me in de Eas' (You may bury me in de Wes', but I'll hear de trumpet soun' in dat mornin')

B. Deliverance
By an' By
Children, We All Shall Be Free (when the Lord shall appear)
O Rocks, Don't Fall on Me: Revelation 6:16
Stan' Still Jordan: Joshua 3-4

C. Heaven
All God's Chillun Got Wings
Don't Call de Roll (till I get dere): Revelation 20:12-15
Going to Heaven (to see that bleedin' Lam'): Revelation 5:6
Gwine Up: 1 Thessalonians 4:13-18
I Am Seekin' for a City (Lord, I don't feel no-ways tired): Hebrews 13:14
I Want God's Hebben to Be Mine
I Want to Be Ready (to walk in Jerusalem jus' like John)
I'll Be There in the Mornin' (when the gen'ral roll is called)
I'm Gwine up to Hebben Anyhow
I've Been Toilin' at de Hill (so long, an' about t'git t'hebben at las')
I've Got a Mother in de Heaven (outshines de sun, way beyond de moon)
In Bright Mansions Above: John 14:2
Oh, When I Git t' Heaven
Oh, Yes! Oh, yes! Wait 'Til I Git on My Robe: Revelation 6:11; 7:9-14
Roll, Jordan, Roll
Run, Mary, Run (I know de oder worl' am not like dis)
Sweet Canaan (de land I am bound for)
To See God's Bleedin' Lam' (want to go to hebben, when I die, when I die)

Want to Go to Heaven When I Die

When the General Roll Is Called (I'll be there): Revelation 20:12

Where Shall I Be When de Firs' Trumpet Soun'?: 1 Thessalonians 4:16

D.   Judgment

Babylon's Fallin': Revelation 14:8; 18:10, 20

Dere's a Han'writin' on de Wall: Daniel 5:5

Dere's No Hidin' Place down Dere: Psalm 139:8; Revelation 6:15-16

Go, Mary, an' Toll de Bell

Great Day

In dat Great Gittin' up Mornin' (fare you well)

Sweet Turtle Dove (Jerusalem Mornin')

Judgment (Judgment Day is a-rollin' a-round)

My Lord Says He's Gwineter Rain down Fire: Revelation 20:9

My Lord, What a Mornin' (when de stars begin to fall): Mark 13:25; Revelation 6:13

My Lord's A-Writin' (A-Ridin') All the Time

Oh, the Rocks and the Mountains: Revelation 6:16

Put John on de Islan': Revelation 1:9

You Goin' to Reap Jus' What You Sow: Galatians 6:7

III.   Biblical Themes

Daniel Saw de Stone: Daniel 2:34-35

De Band o' Gideon: Judges 7:8

De Blin' Man Stood on de Road an' Cried: Mark 10:46-52

De Ol' Ark's A-Moverin' an' I'm Going Home: Genesis 7:17

Father Abraham (sittin' down side ob de Holy Lam')

John Saw the Holy Number: Revelation 7:9

Lit'le David Play on Yo' Harp: 1 Samuel 16:23

Mary an' Martha Jes' Gone 'Long: John 11 (to ring dem charmin' [chiming] bells)

Oh, He Raise-a Poor Lazarus: John 11

Peter on the Sea (Drop your nets and follow me): Luke 5:4-11

'Raslin' Jacob: Genesis 32:24

See Fo' an' Twenty Elders (on de'r knees): Revelation 4:10; 5:8, 14

There Were Ten Virgins: Matthew 25:1-13

'Zekiel Saw de Wheel: Ezekiel 1:16

IV.   Invitation
      Come Down, Sinner, Yo' None Too Late
      Come Here, Lord (sinner cryin')
      De Gospel Train (Git on board, little children)
      Ef You Want to Get to Hebben (come along, come along)
      O Gambler, Git up off o' Yo' Knees
      Oh, Sinner, You'd Better Get Ready (Time is a-comin' dat
         sinner must die)
      Somebody's Knockin' At Yo' Do': Revelation 3:20
      View de Land
      What Yo' Gwine to Do When Yo' Lamp Burn Down? (Oh,
         po' sinner, now is yo' time): Matthew 25:8
      Who'll Jine de Union?
      You Got a Right (. . . to de tree of life): Revelation 22:14

V.   Church
      All I Do, de Church Keep A-Grumblin'
      De Church of God (dat sound so sweet)
      'Tis the Ole Ship of Zion
      We Are Building on a Rock: Matthew 16:18

VI.   Jesus Christ

    A. Birth and Childhood*
        Go Tell It on de Mountain
        Li'l Boy (How ole is you?)
        Mary Had a Baby, Yes, Lord: Matthew 1:25; Luke 2:7
        Rise up, Shepherd, an' Foller: Luke 2:15

    B. The Crucifixion
        Calvary
        Crucifixion
        Did You Hear How Dey Crucified My Lord?

* Evidently the birth of Christ made little impression on the slaves; at least, spirituals dealing with His birth or infancy are rare. Some have suggested the doctrine of the virgin birth left them bewildered; or perhaps in those days the sacredness of Christmas was not stressed, and it was a day of gluttony, guzzling and good-times. Of course, today, it's more of a religious day. Perhaps I should say it is more "spiritual," for December is known to be the biggest month of the year for the consumption of alcoholic beverages in America.

The suggestion that appeals most: the slaves thought of Christ as God Almighty, an idea not too easily reconciled with His being just a baby. J. W. Johnson states that "Christmas" spirituals are post-Civil War. Incidentally, the words and music of "Sweet Little Jesus Boy" are by Robert MacGimsey, 1934 copyright. He was a white musician and lawyer, born in Louisiana. Possibly he picked up the melody and words from former slaves.

Look-a How Dey Done My Lord
Were You There When They Crucified My Lord?

C. Resurrection
But He Ain't Comin' Here t' Die No Mo': Romans 6:
10; Hebrews 9:28
De Angel Roll de Stone Away: Matthew 28:2
Do Don't Touch-a My Garment: John 20:17
Dust an' Ashes (Dey crucified my Savior, an' de Lord
shall bear my spirit home. He arose)
Walk, Mary, down de Lane

D. Second Coming (see also Judgment)
Don't You View dat Ship A-Come A-Sailin'?
Oh, Yes, Yonder Comes My Lord

E. Praise
He Is King of Kings: 1 Timothy 6:15; Revelation 17:
14; 19:16
He's the Lily of the Valley: Song of Solomon 2:1
King Emanuel: Matthew 1:23; Isaiah 7:14
Reign, Massa Jesus
Ride on (King Emanuel. Don't you wan' t'go t'hebben
in de mornin'?)
Ride on, Jesus (Conquerin' King, I want t'go t'hebben
in de mornin')
Why, He's the Lord of Lords (and the King of kings)
Zion, Weep A-Low (Dena Hallelujah to-a de Lamb)

NOTES

Introduction

1. W. E. B. Dubois, *The Souls of Black Folk,* p. xiii.
2. William Pannell states that the major evangelical groups, effectively paralyzed by racism have perpetuated the myth of white supremacy. See his book, *My Friend, The Enemy,* pp. 53, 98.

Chapter 1

1. A. T. Houghton, "Animism" in *The World's Religions,* ed. J. N. D. Anderson, pp. 23-24.
2. John H. Franklin, *From Slavery to Freedom,* p. 57.
3. Kyle Haselden, *Mandate for White Christians,* pp. 32-33; E. Franklin Frazier, *The Negro Church in America,* p. 20; Lerone Bennett, Jr., *Before the Mayflower,* p. 36.
4. Arthur H. Fauset, *Black Gods of the Metropolis,* p. 2.
5. William H. Grier and Price M. Cobbs, *Black Rage,* p. 22.
6. Joseph R. Washington, *Black Religion,* p. 177. See also Frank Tannenbaum, "Slavery Takes Root in the Americas" in *Black History, A Reappraisal,* ed. M. Drimmer, pp. 56-131.

Chapter 2

1. W. D. Weatherford's *American Churches and the Negro,* is an excellent treatment of the work and attitudes of the Episcopal, Quaker, Methodist, Baptist, Lutheran, Presbyterian, Congregationalist, Roman Catholic, and other denominational churches in various states with respect to the Negro during slavery.
2. Andrew E. Murray, *Presbyterians and the Negro—A History.*
3. Carter G. Woodson, *History of the Negro Church,* pp. 41 f.
4. Weatherford, p. 114.
5. Ruby F. Johnston, *The Development of Negro Religion,* pp. 20-21.

Chapter 3

1. Paul Laurence Dunbar, *The Complete Poems of Paul Laurence Dunbar,* pp. 20-23.
2. W. E. B. DuBois, *The Souls of Black Folk,* p. 147.
3. Carter G. Woodson, *The Education of the Negro Prior to 1861,* pp. 202 f.
4. See Josiah Priest, *Bible Defence of Slavery.*
5. C. H. Oliver, *No Flesh Shall Glory* (1959), chaps. 3 and 4, on the significance and biblical history of Shem, Ham, and Japheth, pp. 29-57.
6. James O. Buswell, *Slavery, Segregation and Scripture,* p. 64.
7. Howard Thurman, *Jesus and the Disinherited,* pp. 30-31.
8. Gerhard Kittel, ed., *Theological Dictionary of the New Testament,* 1: 272-73.

Chapter 4

1. *The American Heritage Dictionary of the English Language* (New York: American Heritage, 1969); R. N. Dett, ed., *Religious Folk-Songs of the Negro*, p. xi.

2. One is surprised to learn that "every church, particularly in the South, was much more active in preaching the Gospel to the slaves before 1860 than it has ever been since the Civil War in making Christian teaching available to all the Negro population. . . . The gradual loss of interest on the part of white people in the welfare of the Negro is one of the tragic aspects of the post Civil War period. Many of the churches struggled valiantly to maintain interest in the religious life of the colored people; but the tide was against them" (W. D. Weatherford, *American Churches and the Negro*, pp. 248-49).

3. Kenneth K. Bailey, *Southern White Protestantism*, p. 5.

4. Booker T. Washington, *Up from Slavery*, p. 82. For more information about the religious activities and customs of the Freedmen, see Henderson H. Donald, *The Negro Freedman*, pp. 110-33.

5. Kyle Haselden, *Mandate for White Christians*, p. 29.

6. Kenneth Clark, "The Present Dilemma of the Negro," *The Journal of Negro History*, 53 (1968): 4.

7. W. E. B. DuBois, *The Souls of Black Folk*, pp. 142-43.

8. Ibid., pp. 108-9.

9. E. Franklin Frazier, *The Negro Church in America*, p. 33.

10. Joseph T. Bayly, *Eternity* (Nov. 1962), p. 43.

11. Donald, pp. 179-90.

12. DuBois, pp. 133 f.

13. Washington, p. 78.

14. Ibid., p. 83.

15. Among these schools are the following:

Baptist Schools: Spelman Seminary, begun in 1881 in the basement of the Friendship Baptist Church, Atlanta, Ga.; Virginia Union University in Richmond, Va., 1865; Shaw University, Raleigh, N.C., 1865; Benedict College, Columbia, S. C., 1870; Bishop College, Marshall, Tex., 1880; and Storer College, Harper's Ferry, W. Va., 1867.

Congregational Schools: Fisk, Nashville, Tenn., 1866; Talladega College, Talladega, Ala., 1867; Tougaloo University, Mississippi; Howard University, Washington, D. C., 1867.

Methodist Schools: Meharry Medical School, Nashville, Tenn., 1867; Clark College, Atlanta, Ga., 1869; Claflin University, Orangeburg, S. C., 1869; Bennett College, Greensboro, N. C., 1873; Gammon Theological Seminary, Atlanta, Ga., 1883; Morgan College, Baltimore, Md., 1867.

African Methodist Episcopal: Wilberforce University, Wilberforce, O., 1856; Morris Brown College, Atlanta, Ga., 1881; Allen University, Columbia, S.C., 1870.

African Methodist Episcopal Zion: Livingstone College, Salisbury, N.C., 1879.

Presbyterian: Lincoln University, Oxford, Pa., 1854.

There were also Episcopal schools and independent schools, as well as state educational institutions: Tuskegee, Tuskegee, Ala., 1881; Hampton Institute, Hampton, Va., 1868. Some of these and countless other schools, academies, institutes, colleges and universities were founded by whites, some by blacks; and although most were managed by whites, some were supervised by Negroes.

16. DuBois, pp. 144 f.; and Frazier, pp. 43-44.

Chapter 5

1. C. E. Lincoln, "The Black Muslims as a Protest Movement" in *Black History, A Reappraisal*, Melvin Drimmer, ed., p. 457.

2. Joseph R. Washington, *Black Religion,* p. 53.

3. E. Franklin Frazier, *The Negro Church in America,* p. 51.

4. Preston N. Williams, "Black Church: Origin, History, Present Dilemmas," *Andover-Newton Quarterly* (Nov. 1968), pp. 120-21.

5. Arthur Huff Fauset, *Black Gods of the Metropolis,* Table 3, p. 121.

6. H. A. Ironside, *Galatians,* pp. 137-38.

7. Donald G. Barnhouse, *God's Glory,* Ro. 16:1-2, pp. 122-23.

8. Washington, p. 122; and Frazier, p. 57.

9. See Ruth Boaz, "My Thirty Years with Father Divine," *Ebony* (May 1965), pp. 88-98.

10. Walter Martin, *The Kingdom of the Cults,* chap. 8: "The Reign of Father Divine," p. 218.

11. Philadelphia *Inquirer* (Sept. 11, 1965).

12. Philadelphia *Evening Bulletin* (Sept. 11, 1965).

13. Martin, pp. 220 f.

14. Recorded in the *New Day,* official paper of the Father Divine Movement (Sept. 28, 1968), p. 16.

15. Martin, p. 220.

16. See "Identity Crisis," *Newsweek* (June 30, 1969), p. 62.

17. Lincoln, *The Black Muslims in America,* p. 51. E. U. Essien-Udom's *Black Nationalism: A Search for an Identity in America* is a very thorough treatment of the Black Muslims; for more information about the Moorish-Americans, see pp. 46-48. Also see Fauset, pp. 41-51.

18. *Time* (Mar. 31, 1961), p. 14.

19. *Philadelphia Sunday Bulletin* (Jan. 24. 1965), p. 8.

20. Melvin Drimmer, ed., *Black History: A Reappraisal,* p. 476. In February, 1969, three armed gunmen forced their way into the South Shore home of Raymond D. Sharieff, son-in-law of Elijah Muhammad, and relieved Sharieff of $23,000 in cash as well as valuable jewelry.

21. Malcolm X, "Letters from Mecca" in *The Black Power Revolt,* ed. Floyd B. Barbour, pp. 287-89.

22. Essien-Udom, p. 342.

23. C. Herbert Oliver, *No Flesh Shall Glory,* p. 25.

Chapter 6

1. "Civil Disobedience," editorial, *Christianity Today* 826 (June 5, 1970): 26.

2. Nor in Nebuchadnezzar's realm; read Dan 3, concerning the three Hebrew youths and their deliverance from the fiery furnace.

3. See also August Meier, "On the Role of M. L. King" in *Black History: A Reappraisal,* Melvin Drimmer, ed., pp. 442-54.

4. *U.S. News & World Report* (July 11, 1966), p. 52.

5. James H. Cone, *Black Theology and Black Power,* pp. 6, 8.

6. C. Freeman Sleeper, *Black Power and Christian Responsibility,* p. 193.

7. Preston Williams, "Ethnic Pluralism or Black Separatism?" *Social Progress* (Sept.-Oct. 1969), p. 37.

8. Cone, pp. 6, 8.

9. It is an expression of "no-win fatalism," states Kenneth B. Clark, "The Present Dilemma of the Negro," *The Journal of Negro History* 53 (1968): 8.

10. Robert W. Terry, *For Whites Only,* pp. 14-15.

11. Geddes Hanson, "Black Theology and Protestant Thought," *Social Progress* (Sept.-Oct. 1969), p. 37.

12. Bayard Rustin, "The Myths of the Black Revolt," *Ebony* (Aug. 1969), p. 101.

Chapter 7

1. David O. Moberg, *Inasmuch,* p. 18.
2. "Challenge to Our Churches," photo-editorial, *Ebony* (Mar. 1966), p. 112.
3. John P. Davis, ed., *The American Negro Reference Book,* p. 409.
4. Indeed, 1 Co 9:22 must not be taken out of context: "I am made all things to all men, that I might by all means *save* some."
5. L. Nelson Bell, "A Layman and His Faith: Church Pronouncements," *Christianity Today* 787 (June 20, 1960): 19.
6. See "The Unorthodox Ministry of Leon Sullivan," *Ebony* (May 1971), pp. 112-20.

Chapter 8

1. Joseph R. Washington, *Black Religion,* pp. 151-52.
2. L. L. Berry, *A Century of Missions of the African Methodist Episcopal Church, 1840-1940.*
3. William J. Harvey, III, "The Contribution of the National Baptist Convention to Foreign Missions," *The Mission Herald* 71, No. 7 (Oct.-Nov. 1968): 5, 6, 12. Dr. Harvey is the executive secretary.
4. Ibid., p. 12.
5. The Lott Carey Baptist Foreign Mission Convention, *Lott Carey. . . Fifty-Five Years of Ceaseless Service to Others* (Washington, D.C.: 1953).
6. William E. Pannell, *My Friend, the Enemy,* p. 98.
7. Howard O. Jones, *For This Time,* pp. 111-17.
8. Dick Hillis, "The Missing Black Missionary," *World Vision Magazine* (Jan. 1969), p. 15. A slightly different version of this paragraph is found in Jones, p. 117. See also "America's Black Power in Asia," *World Vision Magazine* (May 1969), p. 43. This article is about Bob Harrison.
9. See Appendix B for a list of more than 200 spirituals.
10. William H. Grier and P. M. Cobbs, *Black Rage,* p. 103.
11. Leonard L. Haynes, Jr., *The Negro Community: Within American Protestantism, 1619-1844,* p. 70. Haynes gives this slant: "In some cases the slave master was unfriendly to the white minister, and forbade the Negroes to attend the meetings. The Negro leader [on the plantation] would disguise his notice to the Negroes that a meeting was to be held thus"—and this spiritual would be sung.
12. Ruby F. Johnston, *The Development of Negro Religion,* p. 30.
13. James Weldon Johnson and J. Rosamond Johnson, *The Books of American Negro Spirituals,* Book 2, p. 12.
14. G. D. Pike, *The Singing Campaign for 10,000 Pounds,* pp. 205-6.
15. J. Garfield Owens, *All God's Chillun,* pp. 10-11. I think Dr. Owens is in error when he claims the spirituals contained "strong elements of resentment, bitterness, revenge, and protest," and when he denies there is any predominantly otherworldliness in the spirituals.
16. Benjamin E. Mays, *The Negro's God: As Reflected in His Literature,* p. 24.
17. E. Franklin Frazier, *Black Bourgeoisie,* p. 118.
18. *Tuesday* (Feb. 1969), p. 12.
19. See *Ebony* (Nov. 1968), p. 74.
20. Washington, pp. 51-52.
21. *Time* (Apr. 28, 1961), p. 72.
22. See "The Beat of Popular Music and the Song of Faith," editorial, *Christianity Today* (Sept. 25, 1961).
23. *Daily Advance,* Lynchburg, Va. (Aug. 7, 1963), p. 3.
24. *Tuesday* (Feb. 1969), p. 12.
25. *Time* (May 23, 1969), p. 52; see also *Newsweek* (May 19, 1969), p. 117.
26. The Reverend King A. Butler, Kalamazoo, Mich. (Nov. 21, 1969).

27. Said the Reverend Bryant M. Kirkland: "What makes music sacred is not a rigid category nor a fixed pattern of taste. The sole criterion is whether or not the musician and the listeners are offered in response and devotion to God," "Jazz Goes to Church," *Ebony* (Apr. 1966), p. 77.

28. *Ebony* (Apr. 1966), p. 80.

29. Don Hustad, "Jazz in the Church," *Eternity* (Apr. 1966), p. 37.

30. Many blacks are offended when told jazz has a pagan origin. It is difficult for me to disagree with those who see in jazz the tom-tom beat of the jungle, and akin to the wailings of voodooists and devil worshipers—claims of a pure art form and cultural contribution notwithstanding. See "Jazz in the Churches: Witness or Weakness?" *Christianity Today* (Mar. 28, 1960), 27 (547).

31. Lee G. Olson, "Music in the Worship Service," *The Alliance Witness,* 103, no. 14 (July 3, 1968): 4.

32. Beveridge said, "Whether in prayer, praise, or preaching, it is the words that make worship uniquely Christian, and it is primarily through the meaning of the words that people come to understand the meaning of Christian symbols and sacraments" (Lowell P. Beveridge, "Church Music: Pop or Pro?" *Christianity Today* 528 [Mar. 14, 1969]: 8).

33. Read W. H. R. Powell's *Illustrations from a Supervised Life* (Philadelphia: Continental, 1968), to see the hand of God in the life of one of the finest Negro ministers produced by God in this country.

34. Arnold J. Toynbee, *A Study of History,* p. 129.

Chapter 9

1. See W. D. Weatherford, *American Churches and the Negro,* pp. 222-45.

2. Joseph R. Washington, *Black Religion,* p. 227.

3. Philadelphia *Evening Bulletin* (Mar. 2, 1969).

4. *Church and State* magazine (Feb. 1969), p. 4.

5. See "Should White Gospel Worker Marry Negro?" *Sword of the Lord* (Sept. 5, 1969), p. 8; and "A White Woman's View of Interracial Marriage," *Sword of the Lord* (Oct. 24, 1969), p. 4.

6. C. H. Oliver, *No Flesh Shall Glory,* p. 86.

7. Kenneth Clark, *Dark Ghetto,* pp. 177-78.

8. Preston Williams, *Andover-Newton Quarterly* (Nov. 1968), p. 123. See also Robert Lee and Ralph L. Roy, "The Negro Church," *Christian Century* (Oct. 30, 1957), pp. 1285-87.

9. See E. Franklin Frazier, *Black Bourgeoisie,* p. 129.

10. William J. Petersen, "Evangelicals and the Race Barriers," *Eternity* (Sept. 1963), p. 13.

11. William H. Grier and Price M. Cobbs, *Black Rage,* pp. 165-66.

BIBLIOGRAPHY

Anderson, J. N. D., ed. *The World's Religions*. Grand Rapids: Eerdmans, 1963.

Bailey, Kenneth K. *Southern White Protestantism*. New York: Harper & Row, 1964.

Barbour, Floyd B., ed. *The Black Power Revolt*. New York: Collier Books, 1969.

Barnhouse, Donald G. *God's Glory*. Grand Rapids: Eerdmans, 1964.

Bennett, Lerone Jr. *Before the Mayflower—A History of the Negro in America 1619-1964,* rev. ed. Baltimore: Penguin Books, 1969 reprint.

Berry, L. L. *A Century of Missions of the African Methodist Episcopal Church, 1840-1940*. New York: Gutenberg, 1942.

Buswell, James O. *Slavery, Segregation and Scripture*. Grand Rapids: Eerdmans, 1964.

Clark, Kenneth B. *Dark Ghetto*. New York: Harper & Row, 1965.

————. "The Present Dilemma of the Negro," *The Journal of Negro History* 53 (1968): 1-11.

Cone, James H. *Black Theology and Black Power*. New York: Seabury, 1969.

Davis, John P., ed. *The American Negro Reference Book*. Englewood Cliffs, N.J.: Prentice-Hall, 1966.

Dett, R.N., ed. *Religious Folk-Songs of the Negro*. Hampton, Va.: Hampton Institute, 1927.

Donald, Henderson H. *The Negro Freedman*. New York: Schuman, 1952.

Drimmer, Melvin, ed. *Black History: A Reappraisal*. Garden City, N. Y.: Doubleday, 1968.

Du Bois, W. E. B. *The Souls of Black Folk*. Greenwich, Conn.: Fawcett, 1964 reprint.

————. *The Suppression of the African Slave-Trade to the U.S.A. 1638-1970*. New York: Schocken Books, 1969. (1896).

Dunbar, Paul Lawrence. *The Complete Poems of Paul Lawrence Dunbar,* New York: Dodd, Mead, 1960.

Essien-Udom, E. U. *Black Nationalism: A Search for an Identity in America.* New York: Dell, 1964.

Fauset, Arthur Huff. *Black Gods of the Metropolis.* Philadelphia: U. Pennsylvania, 1944.

Franklin, John Hope. *From Slavery to Freedom.* New York: Knopf, 1956.

Frazier, E. Franklin. *Black Bourgeoisie.* New York: Free Press, 1957.

————. *The Negro Church in America.* New York: Schocken Books, 1963.

Grier, William H. and Cobbs, Price M. *Black Rage.* New York: Basic Books, 1968.

Haselden, Kyle. *Mandate for White Christians.* Richmond: John Knox, 1966.

Haynes, Leonard L. *The Negro Community: Within American Protestantism, 1619-1844.* Boston: Christopher, 1953.

Ironside, H. A. *Galatians.* New York: Loizeaux, 1940.

Johnson, James Weldon and Johnson, J. Rosamond. *The Books of American Negro Spirituals.* New York: Viking, 1969.

Johnston, Ruby F. *The Development of Negro Religion.* New York: Philosophical Library, 1954.

Jones, Howard O. *For This Time.* Chicago: Moody, 1968.

Kittel, Gerhard, ed. *Theological Dictionary of the New Testament.* Vol. 2. Grand Rapids: Eerdmans, 1964.

Lincoln, C. Eric. *The Black Muslims in America.* Boston: Beacon, 1961.

Loescher, Frank S. *The Protestant Church and the Negro—A Pattern of Segregation.* New York: Association, 1948.

Logan, Rayford W. *The Negro in the U.S.* Princeton: Van Nostram, 1957.

Martin, Walter. *The Kingdom of the Cults.* Grand Rapids: Zondervan, 1965.

Mays, Benjamin E. *The Negro's God: As Reflected in His Literature.* New York: Negro Universities, 1969.

Moberg, David O. *Inasmuch.* Grand Rapids: Eerdmans, 1965.

Murray, Andrew E. *Presbyterians and the Negro—A History.* Philadelphia: Presbyterian Historical Soc., 1966.

Oliver, C. Herbert. *No Flesh Shall Glory.* Nutley, N. J.: Presbyterian & Reformed, 1959.

Owens, J. Garfield. *All God's Chillun.* Nashville: Abingdon, 1971.

Pannell, William E. *My Friend, The Enemy.* Waco, Tex.: Word, 1968.

Pike, Gustavus D. *The Singing Campaign for 10,000 Pounds.* New York: Amer. Missionary Assn., 1875.

Priest, Josiah. *Bible Defence of Slavery.* Detroit: Negro History Press, n.d. (1853).

Singleton, George A. *The Romance of African Methodism.* New York: Exposition, 1952.

Skinner, Tom. *Black and Free.* Grand Rapids: Zondervan, 1968.

Sleeper, C. Freeman. *Black Power and Christian Responsibility.* Nashville: Abingdon, 1969.

Terry, Robert W. *For Whites Only.* Grand Rapids: Eerdmans, 1970.

Thurman, Howard. *The Negro Spiritual Speaks of Life and Death.* New York: Harper, 1947.

————. *Jesus and the Disinherited.* New York: Abingdon-Cokesbury, 1949.

Toynbee, Arnold J. *A Study of History.* New York: Oxford U., 1947.

Washington, Booker T. *Up from Slavery.* Boston: Houghton Mifflin, 1928.

Washington, Joseph R. *Black Religion.* Boston: Beacon, 1964.

Weatherford, W.D. *American Churches and the Negro.* Boston: Christopher, 1957.

Williams, Preston N. "Black Church: Origin, History, Present Dilemmas," *Andover-Newton Quarterly* (Nov. 1968).

Woodson, Carter G. *The Education of the Negro Prior to 1861.* Washington, D.C.: Assn. for the Study of Negro Life and History, 1919.

————. *History of the Negro Church.* Washington, D.C.: Associated Publishers, 1921.

SUBJECT INDEX

SCRIPTURE INDEX

159